In the Name of Allah, the Beneficent, the Merciful

ISLAMIZATION OF KNOWLEDGE SERIES (2)

To Nadio Bhai,

With Best Regards.

Khalid. S. Ahmad.

London
sept 86.

Toward
Islamic
Anthropology

DEFINITION, DOGMA, AND DIRECTIONS

Akbar S. Ahmed

Director General, National Center for Rural Development, and
Director, Center of Social Sciences and Humanities, University Grants
Commission, Islamabad, Pakistan

NEW ERA PUBLICATIONS

© International Institute of Islamic Thought, 1986

Published by
NEW ERA PUBLICATIONS
P.O. Box 8139, 221 Felch Street, Ann Arbor, MI 48103 U.S.A.

Distribution by
AL-QUDS PUBLICATIONS
Crown House, Crown Lane, East Burnham, Bucks, SL2 3SG, England

SAUDI PUBLISHING HOUSE
Al-Jauhara Building, 2nd Floor
Baghdadia, P.O. Box 2043. JEDDAH, Saudi Arabia

ISBN 0-912463-05-8
Library of Congress Catalog Card Number: 85-082303

ACKNOWLEDGMENT

Dr. Muhammad Afzal and Professors Khurshid Ahmad and Isma'īl al Faruqi are warmly acknowledged for their assistance in this study. In particular, Professor al Faruqi has been a constant source of inspiration in encouraging me to write on Islam and Islamic anthropology.

In order to reflect Western anthropology faithfully, I have borrowed extensively from a leading British anthropologist, Professor H. Beattie, for the sections dealing with Western Anthropology.

This has been an exploratory exercise. I hope to examine the major issues raised in greater detail in the future.

FOREWORD

THIS is the first of a series of works which the International Institute of Islamic Thought presents to the reader in fulfillment of its program for the Islamization of the sciences. This program, conceived and crystallized in a number of symposia on the subject, consists of twelve steps designed to effect the necessary Islamization in the various disciplines of human knowledge.[1] Some of these steps seek to survey and evaluate modern Western accomplishments. Others do the same for the legacy of Muslim learning. The purpose is to reach full mastery of the "state of the art" in each discipline, and to prepare that discipline for re-establishment on Islamic foundations. This implies correction of its prejudices and errors, elimination of its shortcomings, and redress of its methodology and aspirations. Islamization does not mean subordination of any body of knowledge to dogmatic principles or arbitrary objectives, but liberation from such shackles. Islam regards all knowledge as critical; i.e., as universal, necessary and rational. It wants to see every claim pass through the tests of internal coherence, correspondence with reality, and enhancement of human life and morality. Consequently, the Islamized discipline which we hope to reach in the future will turn a new page in the history of the human spirit, and bring it closer to the truth.

The present study is the first systematic attempt to assess Western anthropology from an Islamic point of view. Its candid conclusion that there is much in that discipline for Islamic scholars to learn and much to avoid coheres with the universality and objectivity of the Islamic spirit that moves the author of this work.

The erroneous conclusions of Western anthropologists which Dr. Akbar Ahmed has exposed in this survey may be staggering both in number and in quality. Those of them which have resulted from misinformation may be regarded as more or less vexing annoyances. The methodological errors, however, are more serious. Methodological prejudice is a challenge which calls upon the Islamic mind to mobilize its resources for combat. Regarding the cause of truth as its own, Islam prescribes that where there is valid evidence for the other point of view, the mind must bend itself to it with humility. But where the evidence is spurious or lacking, the Islamic mind

---

[1] For details of the program see *Islamisation of Knowledge: General Principles and Workplan* (Washington. D.C.: The International Institute of Islamic Thought, 1402/1982).

7

feels itself compelled to expose the incoherence. The truth is exclusivist; it admits of no compromise. And yet, by virtue of its recognition of God as the Source of all truth, the Islamic mind is never arrogant. It never claims finality for its pronouncements, such being the exclusive prerogative of revelation.

As far as the Muslim world is concerned, Western anthropology has revealed many faces. The travellers and explorers of early times, the scientists and generals who accompanied Napoleon to Egypt, the colonial administrators of Muslim provinces, were all "anthropologists," seeking to study social reality in order to subject it to the desiderata of colonialism. The missionaries entrusted with the religion of love and brotherhood and their dependents — namely, the teachers disseminating knowledge and the physicians administering healing medicines — were "anthropologists" seeking to convert quislings and collaborators, or to shake the foundations of Islam in the minds of its adherents. Lastly, the Western social scientists and other professionals of many descriptions — folklorists, historians of art and literature, linguists, ethnomusicologists and their caricatures, the new breed of Western-trained Muslim scholars — are "anthropologists" who have mastered the art of absolutizing native provincial and popular cultures of the masses as the pre-Islamic founts of "national" existence.

The pile of their blunders and prejudgments is colossal and, as Dr. Akbar Ahmed asserts, there is no escape from exposing their mistakes and recasting their knowledge after purification. Whereas those who were unaware of the unconscious service they have been rendering to the neo-colonialist enemy may be excused as "useful simpletons," the others ought to be confronted, and their involvement in the fragmentation which colonialism has inflicted upon the Muslims of the world should be exposed.

The positive direction to which a redressed anthropology may be directed must derive from the vision of Islam. This vision is determined by the unity and transcendence of God, reason, life- and world-affirmation, universalism, ummatism (from *ummah,* the world community) and ethical service as the *raison d'etre* of humanity. Perhaps the most difficult requirement for anthropology today is to comply with the principle of Islamic universalism. Western anthropology has too long been addicted to an ethnocentrist view of reality. It can hardly define man except in terms of ethnic characteristics. Ethnicity itself is taken to be sacrosanct and inviolable, an ultimate reality which determines what is as well as what ought to be. There can be no doubt that ethnicity is a fact of creation, as the Qur'an has described it in 49:13; a fact worthy of study and analysis for the identification, complementation and enrichment effects it brings to human life. But there is equally no doubt that ethnicity must not lead to ethnocentrism, in which all values are subject to it as ultimate principle of being and ethics. That is the predicament of cultural relativism in which most anthropologists have fallen and continue to fall today.

Anthropology, like all disciplined pursuit of knowledge, must pull itself out of this narrow vision to which it has been confined by the necessities of

European history. It should humanize and universalize itself, and stop looking at the peoples of the world as if they were specimens in a zoo, each specimen carrying its own habits or "culture" as an autonomous end in itself, or as instruments for Western dominion, or as a vacuum to be filled by Western religion, culture and civilization. It should learn anew the simple but primordial truths of all knowledge that are equally the first truths of Islam, namely, that truth is one, just as God is one and as humankind is one.

Isma'īl R. al Fārūqī
President,
International Institute of Islamic Thought

Contents

PART ONE

I. Introduction: Page

    A. The Science of Anthropology   13
    B. Anthropology and Other Sciences of Man   19
    C. Anthropology and the Colonial Encounter   25

II. Anthropological Fieldwork   28

III. Theoretical Frames in Western Anthropology   31

    A. Social Structure   32
    B. Kinship and Political Organization   36
    C. Beliefs, Magic and Religion   41
    D. Economic Anthropology   44
    E. Processes of Social Change   48

IV. The Orientalist Anthropologist   50

PART TWO

V. Islamic Anthropology

    A. The Problem of Definition   56
    B. Muslim Societies   61
    C. Society During the Time of the Prophet   64

VI. Conclusion

    A. Recommendations   65
    B. Conclusion   67

PART ONE

INTRODUCTION

A. The Science of Anthropology

This study is speculatory and concerns a difficult and complex subject. Its task is made more difficult as it defends a metaphysical position, advances an ideological argument and serves a moral cause. It will, therefore, remain an incomplete part of an on-going process in the debate on key issues in contemporary Muslim society.

The major task of anthropology[1] — the study of man — is to enable us to understand ourselves through understanding other cultures. Anthropology makes us aware of the essential oneness of man and therefore allows us to appreciate each other. It is only quite recently in history that it has come to be widely accepted that human beings are fundamentally alike; that they share basic interests, and so have certain common obligations to one another. This belief is either explicit or implicit in most of the great world religions, but it is by no means acceptable today to many people even in "advanced" societies, and it would make no sense at all in many of the less-developed cultures. Among some of the indigenous tribes of Australia, a stranger who cannot prove that he is a kinsman, far from being welcomed hospitably, is regarded as a dangerous outsider and may be speared without compunction. Members of the Lugbara tribe of northwestern Uganda used to think that all foreigners were witches, dangerous and scarcely human creatures who walked about upside-down and killed people by magic. The ancient Greeks believed that all non-Hellenic peoples were barbarians, uncivilised savages whom it would be quite inappropriate to treat as real people. Many citizens of modern states today think of people of other races, nations or cultures in ways which are not very different from these, especially if their skin is differently colored or if they hold other religious or political faiths.

An eminent British anthropologist has noted: "When I was an administrator in Tanzania, it was widely held that Europeans were cannibals, who kidnapped African children and others and processed them for sale as tinned meat. Some European stereotypes about Africans were no less absurd. I have heard Europeans who had lived for many years in Africa

---

1 From *anthropos*, Greek for man.

(but who had never bothered to learn an African language properly, or to get to know any Africans outside the master-servant relationship) assert that Africans are lacking in natural family affections, that they do not know the meaning of gratitude, and that their languages lack a word for "thank you" (Beattie 1977:273).

I do not here discuss in detail the historical development of social anthropology; full accounts are available elsewhere. But it will be easier to see why contemporary social anthropology is the kind of subject it is if we have some idea of what has led up to it. As a branch of empirical, observational science, it grew up in the context of the world-wide human interaction which has vastly increased in the past century. What is most familiar is often taken for granted, and the idea that the study of living human communities was of legitimate scientific interest in its own right became evident when detailed information began to be available about hitherto remote and unfamiliar human societies. These societies had been speculated about since time immemorial, but they could not be scientifically investigated until new, easier and quicker ways of getting about the world made it possible for scholars to visit and observe them.

Initially, the reports of eighteenth- and nineteenth-century missionaries and travellers in Africa, North America, the Pacific and elsewhere provided the raw material upon which the first western anthropological works, written in the second half of the last century, were based. Before then there had been plenty of conjecturing about human institutions and their origins to say nothing of earlier times in the eighteenth century. Hume, Adam Smith and Ferguson in Britain, and Montesquieu, Condorcet and others on the Continent, had written about primitive institutions. Although their speculations were often brilliant, these thinkers were not empirical scientists; their conclusions were not based on evidence which could be tested. On the contrary, their speculations were deductively argued from principles which were for the most part implicit in their own cultures. They were really philosophers and historians of Europe, not anthropologists as we would now understand the term.

The common view was that civilized men could have nothing profitable to learn from studying the way of life of a lot of savages. It is reported that even at the end of the nineteenth century the famous Sir James Frazer, when asked if he had ever seen one of the primitive people about whose customs he had written so many volumes responded with "God Forbid!" In an important sense these writers were the forerunners of modern social anthropologists.

Modern social anthropology owes much to these nineteenth-century scholars, in spite of their misconceptions. Although they were mainly preoccupied with the reconstruction of a past which was lost forever, they were like their successors, interested in social institutions and the interrelations between the cultural and social institutions of different societies.

By the end of the nineteenth century a considerable amount of miscellaneous ethnographic information had been assembled from all over the world. The most celebrated collection is that of James Frazer. His compilation of religious beliefs and practices was published in several editions around the turn of the century as *The Golden Bough*. In this work Frazer, starting with the idea found in ancient Roman myth that the priest-ruler, as representative of a god, should be slain and replaced by another before his powers waned, collected a vast body of information about "primitive" religious and magical practices throughout the world. Like his predecessors, Frazer was mainly interested in origins, but he did claim that social anthropology (he was one of the first to apply the adjective "social" to the discipline) should seek regularities or general laws. The laws he had in mind, however were those exemplified in the earlier stages of human society, and were represented, so he and the evolutionists believed, by existing "primitive" societies.

Like most of his contemporaries, Frazer was still concerned with isolated "customs", reported from various parts of the world largely by people with little or no scientific training, and so considered apart from the living social contexts that could give them real meaning. Frazer's approach is very different from that of modern social anthropologists. Even so, the literary skill and imaginative sweep of his work caught the imagination of both scholars and the general reader in the West.

As the quantity of ethnographic information increased, and its quality gradually improved, it began to dawn on some scholars that this material was too important to be used merely to illustrate preconceived ideas about primitive peoples or about presumed earlier stages of human society. More and more this extensive ethnography was seen to demand some sort of comparative analysis in its own right. Practical concerns stimulated this interest. Colonial administrators and missionaries began increasingly to see that their work would benefit by an understanding of the social and cultural institutions of the populations they dealt with. Some of the best of the earlier monographs on the simpler societies were written by serving missionaries and administrative officers and will be discussed below.

Aided by the colonial enterprise at the turn of the century, there began to develop a scientific concern with a systematic undertaking of first-hand field studies of human communities that had hitherto been known to scholars only through the piecemeal observations of non-professional observers. Individual field studies, a few of very high quality, had been made earlier. Franz Boas's research among the Eskimos in the 1880's was a notable example, and so was Morgan's work among the Iroquois Indians, undertaken more than a generation before. But it was in the early 1900's that the systematic collection of information in the field, covering a wide segment of the social and cultural life of particular peoples, came to be generally regarded as an essential part of the social anthropologist's task. An important stimulus in British anthropology was the Torres Straits expedition in 1898, in which a team of anthropologists led by A.C. Haddon undertook a comprehensive field survey of a part of Melanesia. Later, Radcliffe-Brown's study of the Andaman Islanders, undertaken before the first World War, and Malinowski's work in the Trobriand Islands of the western Pacific during World War I, became particularly important influences in modern social anthropology.

It was with the change of interest from the reconstruction of past societies to the investigation of contemporary societies that modern social anthropology began. From this time forward social anthropologists were no longer satisfied with the collection of isolated pieces of information about particular customs or institutions, however skillfully these might be woven into theoretical schemes, or however wide-ranging the comparisons based on them. It no longer seemed as worthwhile, as it had to Frazer, to collect huge numbers of examples of totemic practices or first-fruit ceremonies from all periods of history and from all corners of the world. "Primitive societies" had at last come into their own; they were no longer merely a vast storehouse from which all kinds of exotic materials could be drawn by the diligent researcher. It was now recognized that however different they were from the familiar states of western Europe, they were, nonetheless, systematically organized and viable communities. So, for the first time, the question arose: how are these unfamiliar social and cultural systems to be understood?

The answer was attempted by French sociological thought with its analytical, intellectualist tradition. Eighteenth- and nineteenth-century French writers about human society were much concerned with the "nature" of society and of human social institutions. Their interest lay rather in what human society essentially is than in the history of its development, either generally or in particular cases. Thus Comte, like his predecessor and teacher, Saint-Simon, was much concerned with stressing that societies are systems, not just aggregates of individuals. Neither an African tribe nor a university town is just a collection of people any more than a house is just a collection of bricks, or an organism just an aggregate of cells. What makes these entities something more than merely the totality of their component parts is the fact that these parts are related to one another in certain specific and recognizable ways. In the case of human communities, the more or less enduring relationships between different peoples are what we refer to when we speak of societies.

The French thinkers saw that if societies were systems, they must be made up of interrelated parts. They also thought that these parts must be related to one another and to the whole society of which they were parts, in accordance with laws analogous to the laws of nature, which in principle at least, it should be possible to discover. So the understanding of societies, and of Society with a capital "S", like the understanding of the physical organisms with which they were either explicitly or implicitly being compared, was to be achieved by discovering the laws of social organization that operated to maintain the whole structure. This "organismic" approach to the study of human societies has some grave limitations and can be misleading. But it did point to the important truth that the customs and social institutions of human communities are somehow interconnected, and that changes in one part of the system may lead to changes in other parts. When this was understood it became possible to ask, and sometimes even to answer, questions about real human societies — questions which arose less readily so long as the "piecemeal" view of human cultures, which had hitherto been dominant, prevailed. Thus an anthropologist faced with a custom such as mother-in-law avoidance, which is found in many societies far remote from one another, was no longer content merely to record it for purposes of comparison with other apparently similar customs elsewhere. He now asked about the implications of the institution for husband-wife relations, or for the pattern of residence. This "organismic" approach reached its most sophisticated expression in the writings of the French sociologist, Emile Durkheim, who is still one of the most important influences in social anthropology.

My concern here is to stress that the two most important strains from which the fabric of modern social anthropology is woven are the fact-finding, empirical, graphic tradition represented by British and by much German and American anthropology and the "holistic", analytical intellectualism of French social philosophy.

Can we then, at this point, give a preliminary statement of what modern social anthropology is about? Anthropology is by definition the study of man. But no one discipline can possibly study man in all his aspects, though some anthropologists have written as though it could. On the whole, social anthropologists have concentrated on the study of man in his social aspect, that is, in his relationships with other people in living communities. The multifarious dimensions of the social and cultural life of more complex, literate societies have for the most part been left to historians, economists, political scientists, sociologists, and a host of other specialist scholars.

Of course, the anthropologist is interested in people; they are the raw material he works with. As a social anthropologist however, his main concern is with what these people share with other people, the institutionalized aspects of their culture. For this reason social anthropologists are not interested in every social relationship in the societies they study; they concentrate mainly on those which are habitual, relatively enduring features of the societies in which they occur.

The emphasis today is essentially empirical and functional. Contemporary social anthropology is centrally a study of relationships between different kinds of people, and at a higher level of abstraction, of relationships between relationships. Let me make this clear. The social anthropologist is not just interested in the relationship between, for example, a particular chief and a particular subject. He is, as we have just noted, interested in the kinds of relationships between chiefs and subjects that are characteristic of the society being studied, and of which the particular case is an example. Further, he is interested in the implications that the institutionalized chief-subject relationship has for other

17

institutionalized relationships in the society, for example, the relationships between different kinds of kin or the system of land-holding.

We shall find that in modern social anthropology the emphasis is contextual and relational. Recent social anthropology may claim to have contributed most significantly to this kind of contextual understanding in the Western social sciences. But anthropologists are today being increasingly associated with practical problems outside the classroom and their solutions.

The UNO and the governments in the British Commonwealth, the United States, and elsewhere have made much use of trained social anthropologists. They have done this in various ways. First, they have added trained sociologists or social anthropologists to their permanent staffs. Thus the anthropologist becomes a civil servant. As such, his primary business is with practical problems upon which he brings to bear the techniques and special knowledge with which his professional training has equipped him. Government anthropologists have been asked to advise on such matters as labor migration, succession to political authority in particular tribes, and the likely social consequences of proposed land reforms. An anthropologist who takes such a post becomes a sort of anthropological general practitioner.

For anthropologists of practical bent, there is much to be said for such a career, and if a government locates the right employee it is well served. Some African governments have successfully made use of professional social anthropologists in this way. Such employers, whether they are governments, missionaries, or businessmen should allow their anthropologists sufficient leisure to enable them to keep reasonably abreast of current theoretical developments in their field, as well as permitting them wide latitude in their approaches to the problems set for them.

A second way in which a government can make practical use of social anthropology is to employ a professional, on contract for a period of a year or two, to carry out a specific piece of research. This method can work well when a particular problem is considered sufficiently important to justify the expense of full-scale, professional study. An anthropologist, who has made a special study of religious institutions, might be hired to investigate the emergence in a particular area of a separatist movement; or an expert on political organization might be engaged to make a study in a community for which major administrative changes were proposed. The Sudan Government employed the anthropologists, Evans-Pritchard and Nadel, in this way before World War II. For such specialized tasks, governments do best to select experienced and established scholars rather than young anthropologists without previous field experience. First field studies are best controlled and financed through universities or other research bodies, and a social anthropologist on his first tour of field work is still very much a student. If he is to become a full-fledged professional, his supervision should be academic rather than administrative.

A third method by which governments have availed themselves of information provided by anthropological investigations is by supporting, encouraging, or merely tolerating research by workers academically attached to universities or other research-sponsoring bodies.

B. Anthropology and Other Sciences of Man

Social anthropologists study people's customs, social institutions, and values, and the ways in which these are interrelated. They carry out their investigations mainly in the context of contemporary, small-scale communities and their central, though not their only interest, is in systems of social relations. It is useful to say something about social anthropology's relationship to other branches of anthropology, and also to certain other social sciences.

In Britain the term "anthropology" loosely designates a number of different branches of study which are more or less closely associated, although sometimes the association derives rather from the historical fact that they developed together as "evolutionary" studies of man and were originally taught together, than from an intrinsic relationship. Thus physical anthropology, prehistoric archaeology, primitive technology, ethnology, and ethnography are usually subsumed with social anthropology under the rubric, anthropology, which sociology is not, even though its problems and methods overlap to a considerable degree with those of social anthropology. So, it is not a bit surprising that the word "anthropology" means different things to different people. Even when it is qualified by the adjective "social", anthropology still suggests to some people an interest in bones and head measurements, to others a concern with prehistoric man and his works, to yet others an obsessive interest in exotic, preferably sexual, customs. Because of the confusion which the ambiguity of the word "anthropology" has caused, perhaps it would be a good thing if another name could be found for the subject we are concerned with. Unfortunately, no one has yet been able to suggest a better one.

Let us discuss briefly the present relationship between social anthropology, as the subject is understood in Britain and the Commonwealth, and some other kinds of anthropology, namely, physical anthropology, prehistoric archaeology or prehistory, ethnography and ethnology, and cultural anthropology. I will then consider its relationship with history and psychology. Social anthropology has some concern with other branches of knowledge too, political science, economics, human geography, agronomy, even philosophy and theology, to name a few. This relationship is not surprising, since social anthropologists claim to take at least some account of the whole social and cultural lives of the peoples they study, and all of these disciplines are concerned with aspects of human culture. Although social anthropology often borrows from, and sometimes lends to these other studies, the borderline between them and anthropology is not a matter of ambiguity or disagreement. In the case of the subjects discussed in this section, however, the link with social anthropology is not

19

only close, but it is also often confused and sometimes disputed.

On the European continent anthropology means physical anthropology. This discipline is concerned with man as a physical organism, and with his place in the scheme of biological evolution. It deals with such topics as the classification of early forms of man, the physical differences between the races of the species, Homo sapiens, human genetics, and the modes of physiological adaptation and reaction to different physical environments. This study is important and interesting, but it has little to do with the analysis of people's social institutions and beliefs.

It is now usual, at least in Britain, to distinguish ethnography from ethnology. The term "ethnography" refers to descriptive accounts of human societies, usually of those simpler, smaller-scale societies which anthropologists have frequently studied. In this sense ethnography may be said to be the raw material of social anthropology. However, descriptive studies imply some generalisation and comparison, either explicit or implicit.

The term "ethnology" was formerly used as a kind of blanket term to designate almost all of the anthropological studies, including physical anthropology and prehistory. It is still sometimes so used in America and on the Continent. But British social anthropologists have found it useful to restrict it to studies of the preliterate people and cultures which attempt to explain their present in terms of their remote past. In this sense, ethnology is the science which classifies people in terms of their racial and cultural characteristics, and attempts to explain these by reference to their history or to their prehistory. To take a concrete example, investigations into the origin of a particular type of canoe are ethnological investigations, while inquiries about its contemporary use and its practical and symbolic significance for the people who have it fall within the scope of social anthropology.

Nowadays a distinction is often drawn, as I have already indicated, between social anthropology and cultural anthropology. Culture has been variously defined, since Sir Edward Tylor described it nearly a century ago, as "that complex whole which includes knowledge, belief, art, morals, law, custom and other capabilities and habits acquired by man as a member of society". In this broadest sense, "culture" refers to the whole range of human activities which are learned and not instinctive, and which are transmitted from generation to generation through various learning processes. Often the physical products of human activity are included under the term as "material culture". Thus understood, cultural anthropology obviously covers an exceedingly broad field, including practically all the nonbiological aspects of human life. Men's social institutions and values, social anthropology's central concerns, occupy only a small part of this range.

To study this whole range of activity would be difficult and most British social anthropologists consider "culture" too extended a concept to be designated a specific field for systematic study. A century ago one scholar

20

might have been able to deal with the whole life of man, at least of "primitive" man, on this massive scale; advances in anthropological knowledge and techniques have made it impossible now. In fact, cultural anthropology has broken down into many specialist fields such as linguistics, acculturation and personality studies, ethnomusicology, and the study of primitive art. On the whole, American scholars have laid more stress on cultural than on social anthropology, which some of them have regarded as a more restricted interest concerned mainly with "social structure". The broader view of the content of the subject has led to a wide dispersal of interest over a variety of fields, such as acculturation studies and learning theory, many of which have been little developed in British anthropology. The broader view has also involved a concern with particular aspects or items of culture, with what have been called "culture traits" rather than with the analysis of cultures or societies as systematic wholes. Much American anthropology is nearer to ethnology, as defined above, than it is to social anthropology as it is understood in Britain.

In America the concern with items of culture rather than with social systems may be partly due to the nature of the ethnographic material most readily available to scholars in that country. Most British social anthropology is based on field studies of people whose societies are still "going concerns", such as island populations in the Pacific and tribal societies in Africa. Until recently American researchers have had much less access to such live material. Many (though by no means all) of the North American Indian groups among which American anthropologists worked had long ago ceased to exist as viable societies, although their members often preserved extensive knowledge of their traditional cultures. In America problems of social and political organisation could not present themselves with the same urgency as they did in the study of the still viable societies of Africa and the Pacific. Thus less work has been done in America than in Britain and the Commonwealth in the analysis of actual communities as working social systems, the field in which recent British social anthropology has made its main contribution. There are important exceptions to this generalisation, but it is significant that some modern British social anthropologists would claim that they have been more influenced by the writings of American sociologists than by those of American anthropologists.

In America cultural anthropologists emphasize the study of symbols and examine how such symbols explain individual and group behaviour in society. Clifford Geertz, one of the leading American anthropologists, writes of culture, "The concept of culture is essentially a semiotic one. Believing, with Max Weber, that man is an animal suspended in webs of significance he himself has spun, I take culture to be those webs, and the analysis of it to be therefore not an experimental science in search of law but an interpretive one in search of meaning. It is explication I am after, construing social expressions on their surface enigmatical" (Geertz 1973: 5).

In contrast British anthropology, terming itself social anthropology,

21

looks at social structure and organization with a view to explaining society. Following is an example of how these different schools interpret the same society differently.

Clifford Geertz at Princeton and Ernest Gellner at London, two of the most prominent Western anthropologists and both leading their distinct schools of anthropology on either side of the Atlantic, have studied Moroccan society. [1]To the former, society is to be interpreted, [as in his book *Meaning and Order in Moroccan Society* (1979)], through the *suq* (market), and relationships that arise from transactions generated in buying and selling. The market becomes symbolic of relationships in society and helps explain larger societal behavior and society. In contrast, Ernest Gellner, who worked among the Berbers in the Atlas mountains (1969, 1981), found social life is organized on the basis of principles characteristic of segmentary tribal society.

However significant, these differences in approach and their importance can be exaggerated — it must be remembered that for the most part they imply only a difference in emphasis — they do not, or at least they should not, imply that social anthropologists and cultural anthropologists study different subject matter. Whether the observer's main interest is in society or in culture, the reality which he observes, people in relation to one another, is one and not two. Cultural and social anthropologists sometimes ask different kinds of questions, but however we distinguish these, there is a good deal of overlap.

So much for the relationship between social anthropology and other kinds of anthropology. I turn now to its relationship with some other social sciences, first of all with history.

Historians are chiefly interested in the past, whether remote or recent; their business is to discover what has happened and why. On the whole, they are more interested in particular sequences of past events and their conditions, than they are in the general patterns, principles, or laws which these events exhibit.

Although the two disciplines are different, social anthropology has a very close relationship with history in two important ways. First, an anthropologist who aims to achieve as complete an understanding as possible of the present condition of the society can hardly fail to ask how it came to be as it is. Although his central interest is in the present, the past may be directly relevant in explaining the present. In the twenties and thirties some social anthropologists, reacting against the pseudohistorical hypotheses of the preceding generation, went so far as to imply that history

1. In spite of the attack on Jewish scholars — as Zionists — by Edward Said (1978) not all Jewish scholars are Zionist. The most perceptive anthropological work in Morocco has been conducted by those with a Jewish background — however nominal (Brown, C. and H. Geertz, Gellner, Rabinow and Rosen). Is it, as Bernard Lewis suggests, a Jewish sense of affinity for Muslims in relation to Western civilizations within which they live? (*Lewis 1972: 35-6*). We do know from these studies that Jewish groups live in harmony with the majority Muslims in Morocco.

could never be relevant for social anthropologists, whose proper concern was with structural relations not with historical ones. Some of Radcliffe-Brown's earlier writings expressed this view, though he later repudiated it. Few social anthropologists today adopt so extreme an approach. Many of them have worked in relatively advanced communities that have documented histories. Also, European contact and the changes which have followed from it have provided histories, not always happy ones, for societies which formerly had none. So, most modern social anthropologists do take account of the histories of the societies they study, where historical material is available and where it is relevant to the understanding of the present.

Second, the study of social change is by definition a historical one, though it makes use of sociological categories as well. Though they are different, the aims and methods of social anthropologists and historians coincide in some degree. Historians use documentary evidence infrequently available to anthropologists, and anthropologists employ first-hand observation rarely possible for historians. Both are concerned with the description and understanding of real human situations, and they use whatever methods are available and appropriate to this purpose. Like historians (and unlike natural scientists) a social anthropologist can make the way of life of the creatures he studies intelligible to us only insofar as he manages to convey to us something of what it would be like to participate in that way of life. His task is largely one of interpretation. An anthropologist who tries to understand why African chiefs in a selected tribe act as they do is not engaged in an enterprise essentially different from that of a historian who is trying to understand why Roman emperors of a particular period acted as they did. Both anthropologists and historians attempt to represent unfamiliar social situations in terms not just of their own cultural categories, but, as far as possible, in terms of the categories of the actors themselves. The main difference between anthropology and history lies not so much in the subject matter (though generally this does differ) as in the degree of generality with which it is dealt. Once again, it is a question of emphasis. Historians are interested in the history of particular institutions in particular places, parliament in England, for example, or the Hapsburg monarchy. But they are also concerned, implicitly if not explicitly, with the nature of these institutions themselves. A social anthropologist who is concerned with the role of chiefs in a particular society must be a historian to the extent of studying the careers and activities of individual chiefs. Unless he does so, his account will be empty, formal, and unconvincing. Although in a general sense historians are concerned with what is individual and unique, and social anthropologists, like sociologists, are concerned with what is general and typical, this dichotomy is too simple. As so often in the social sciences, the difference is largely one of emphasis.

Social anthropology is not psychology, although like sciences which deal with human affairs, it constantly makes use of psychological terms and concepts. Psychology is concerned with the nature and functioning of individual human minds, and although it is generally accepted that human mentality is a product of social conditioning, the study of that mentality differs in important ways from the study of the social and cultural environment which is its context.

Rather, as in the study of history, a tendency to deny that psychology can have any relevance for social anthropology is now being replaced by a recognition of the important contributions it can make to the understanding of people's social behaviour. This recognition is associated with social anthropology's concern with what people think and with their systems of beliefs, symbols, and values. The impact of Freud on social anthropology, as on human thinking generally, has been considerable, though for the most part indirect. His one incursion into anthropology, his theory of the origin of totemism, is hardly convincing, but his massive demonstration of the primacy of symbolic, irrational elements in human thought has had far-reaching influence on the subject.

In fact, every field anthropologist must be to a considerable extent a practicing psychologist. An important part of his job is to discover what the people he is studying think, never a simple task. Ideas and values are not given as data; they must be inferred, and there are many difficulties and dangers in such inferences, particularly when they are made in the context of an unfamiliar culture. It may well be that there is much to be learned through the techniques of depth psychology about the less explicit values of other cultures (as well as about those of our own), especially about the symbolism involved in rituals and ceremonies. But a word of warning is necessary. The incautious application in unfamiliar cultures of concepts and assumptions derived from psychological research in Western society may lead — and indeed has led — to gross distortions. The Oedipus complex, for example, is something to be proved, not assumed, in other cultures. To sum up, the association of psychology with physical anthropology, prehistoric archaeology and prehistory is historical only; today social anthropology has little or no concern with these subjects. It shares its subject matter with ethnology, and with it possesses a common base in ethnography. The questions it asks are not ethnological, but relate rather to contemporary society and culture. Its emphasis differs from that of cultural anthropology, although social anthropologists are concerned with culture too. Anthropologists use history, but for a purpose not itself strictly historical, that is, to understand the present. They also use psychological concepts, though their chief interest is in the society and culture in which individuals participate, rather than in the individuals themselves.

Social anthropologists, more than other social scientists, need to have some acquaintance with the concepts and methods of a number of subjects. The simpler, small-scale societies which they usually study and many of the institutionalised social relationships and values in which they are interested are in fields which in more complex cultures are studied by specialist disciplines. Thus, for example, social anthropologists who study "primitive law" should know at least some of the vocabulary of law and jurisprudence;

those who are concerned with relationships of political power and authority, should know some of the categories of political science, and those interested in production and exchange in the societies they study should know those of economics. The social anthropologist's claim to treat these and other specialized subjects in the context of his own studies is less arrogant than it may seem. The relationships which such subjects comprise are, for the most part, small in scale and relatively simple in content. They are effective on a person-to-person level, and since they are for the most part comprehensible to non-specialist members of the cultures concerned, they are also comprehensible to the anthropologist who has really "learned" the culture. Nor, in the primitive cultures which social anthropologists study, does the understanding of social and cultural institutions require, as it would in literate societies, the mastering of numerous books and documents. Thus when social anthropologists, in the restricted context of the small-scale communities in which they work, investigate the several dimensions of social and cultural life, their investigation does not demand the lengthy specialist training necessary for the study of any one of these dimensions in a complex, literate society.

C. Anthropology and the Colonial Encounter

Modern Anthropology is seen by its Marxist and Third World critics as a product of colonialism which is true to the extent that anthropology and anthropologists have aided the colonial enterprise sometimes overtly and sometimes indirectly.

Ethnographic investigation and colonial enterprise have gone hand in hand from the first. In Bonaparte's expedition to Egypt were 150 scientists including ethnographers with pen and notebook in hand. This first contact between colonizing Europe and colonised Asia or Africa laid the foundation of ethnographic methodology for these continents. The ethnographic interest in colonized people was to culminate in the exhaustive studies of African, Asian and Oceanian society.

The Orientalist (the Western scholar of peoples and customs of the Orient) contributed to the image of the Oriental. During the colonial decades a cumulative picture of the Orient formed in Western minds. Let me cite the author of *Orientalism* for a description of the Oriental, "The Oriental is irrational, depraved (fallen), childlike, 'different' ". In contrast, "the European is rational, virtuous, mature, 'normal' " (Said 1978: 40). Following is a discussion of the Orientalist influence on anthropology.

The colonial period produced some of the most informative ethnographic material on "native" and "primitive" peoples. For instance, some of the most detailed and accurate ethnography on the Pukhtuns comes from the British colonial period. It begins with a colonial officer (Elphinstone 1972) and ends with one (Caroe 1965). Similarly Robert Montagne, a French colonial administrator, is the author of the most rewarding work on the Berbers in Morocco.

Not all colonial ethnography is defective, although its political assumptions are. Sometimes political officers administering tribal groups were more sympathetic to their charges than some of the postcolonial native officials who succeeded them. Perhaps some of these colonial officers were themselves men of sensitivity and perception. These qualities, together with assignments to peripheral provinces of the colonial administrations, made them marginal to the great metropolitan empires. They posed questions difficult to answer in the context of colonialism.[1] Morocco for the French and India for the British were the "jewels" in the colonial crown. It is no coincidence that the best officers were assigned there. Some of them proved to be excellent ethnographers.

A study of their relationship with the cultural system that produced them, and the more traditional one that attracted the colonial officers who administered tribal groups, would be rewarding.[2] It would tell much about the colonial power and also a great deal about the virtues and vices of tribal groups.

In an important sense anthropological writing is auto-biographical. Studies today have illustrated the psychological reasons why "Arabists" — the European traveler-scholars — reacted to the Arabs as they did. Their lineage, schooling, and childhood helped form their reaction. It would be instructive to be aware of the relevant biographical aspects of the anthropologist's life. We might have a more comprehensive picture of the group if we knew the relationship between the author and his subject.

Deeper studies of the famous "Arab" scholar-travelers are now being written.[3] Their relationship to Islam, for instance, obviously determined their attitudes to its adherents. We know that Doughty hated Islam, which to him symbolized everything decadent and corrupt. In contrast, Blunt almost became a Muslim, such was his fascination with Islam. Some officer-scholars were motivated by forces that lay deep in family psychology and childhood memory. For instance, it is widely recognised that T.E. Lawrence, the illegitimate son of a nobleman, attempted to live out his fantasies through his Arabian adventures. He was "getting even" with the world through the Arab legend in a distant land where he had princes at his beck and call. The Lawrence saga is poor historiography but excellent press.

The scholar-travelers wore native clothes and spoke the native language. In their flamboyant behavior and eccentric appearance, they imagined they found acceptance far from home (Burton's moustache which had provoked adverse comment at Oxford was appreciated by tribal chiefs). Rejected in some childhood memory, they would indulge every fantasy in

---

1. One good example of a political officer who sympathised with his tribes and compared their code of behavior favourably to Western civilization was Sir Evelyn Howell (see Ahmed 1980b).

2. My colleague, David Hart, and I are working on a joint volume examining just this perspective, *Islamic Tribes and European Administrators: Readings in the Colonial Encounter* (Ahmed and Hart forthcoming book).

the East. They were not adult men playing at boys, but boys playing at men. Kings and chiefs were made and unmade by them (from Edwardes to Lawrence they prided themselves on this power) and they created grand sounding titles from exotic places for their heroes: Edwardes of Bannu, Gordon of Khartoum, Roberts of Kandahar and Lawrence of Arabia.[1] They were not just Orientalist villains destroying native custom and trampling on native culture. The picture is more complex.

Orientalists were only partly racist; a number of them sought identity among and with tribal groups, and sometimes the former was subordinated to the latter. However, the romance was one-way only.

European colonial scholarship was not politically innocent. Its aim was to understand the colonials better in order to dominate them more efficiently. This knowledge was translated into administrative policy. A crude example may be given from both the British and French colonies.

Determined attempts were made to separate the people of the hills from the people of the plains. Hill tribes were projected as proud, honest, hospitable, egalitarian people abiding by a traditional tribal code. In contrast, groups living in the plains were seen as servile, unreliable, and racially inferior. The former provided the prototype of the noble savage. To the French, the Berbers and to the British, the Pukhtuns fell in the first group.

Translating ethnographic knowledge into administrative reality, the French through the Berbère Dahir in North Africa and the British through the Tribal Areas in north India administratively cut off the hill tribes from their cousins in the low lands. The separate administrative entity, it was hoped, would eventually create an ideological division within the population. We know that in both areas the colonial strategy was not entirely successful.

When it came to resisting the colonial power, hill and plains cousins joined hands. Indeed, the hill tribes, far from accepting the new boundaries, continued to raid into and harass the Imperial districts.

Similarly, and perhaps unconsciously, some modern anthropologists follow the imperial attempt to separate Muslim groups. One means is to distinguish "good" from "poor Moslems". Certain anthropologists go to great lengths to establish that nomad/tribal groups possess "a reputation for being poor Moslems" (Tapper 1979:2). Barth found the Basseri in Iran "poor Moslems" (Barth 1961). There is, however, general though scattered evidence to the contrary (Ahmed 1980 a, 1982 b, Ahmed and Hart 1982, Cole 1975, Lewis 1961).

The link between colonialism and academic anthropology continued

3. For a new and interesting psychological insight into the famous Arabist Western scholar-travellers see Tidrick 1981; for the impressions of Arab women of these very 'Arabists' see Pastner 1978.

1. See "The Man Who Would Be King: British Political Officers among the Bedouin and the Pukhtun" (Ahmed forthcoming paper).

even after the second World War when most Muslim countries were free or almost free of their colonial masters. It is not entirely a coincidence that some of the better known post-war British anthropologists were officers who had held colonial posts in the empire.

Evans-Pritchard, Leach, and Nadel, to name a few eminent British social anthropologists, held colonial posts.[1] Of these the most outstanding was Evans-Pritchard who was a Tribal Affairs Officer in Cyrenaica and who formulated the models based on Bedouin ethnography which were to later become the classic statement for segmentary tribal society. In a sense the segmentary theory had returned home to the Bedouin — for whom Robertson Smith discussed it — after its first major anthropological statement for the Nuer by Evans-Pritchard. Segmentary tribal society, comprised of those tribesmen related to each other genealogically and traced to an apical — and usually eponymous — ancestor, organised in segments with "nesting attributes". These tribes were generally seen as "anarchic" and too primitive for their members to be socially differentiated.

In South Asia the imperial roots of anthropology reach beyond this century. It was Henry Maine, the Law Member of the Viceroy's Council, who with his *Ancient Law* (1861) and *Village Communities in the East and West* (1871) could justifiably claim to have laid the foundations of anthropology — or village studies — in India. Lyall, who was to become the Lieutenant Governor of the North-West provinces, published his *Asiatic Studies: Religious and Social* in 1882. Imperial administrators in the field share with the anthropologist its major characteristic, the fieldwork experience.

II. ANTHROPOLOGICAL FIELDWORK

The work of the anthropologist is to study other cultures. Through them he learns to understand his own culture, and equally important, himself. He remains essentially a seeker. In the distant village and among strange people he comes face to face with himself — a chilling prospect. In that encounter is reflected his true self. His writing too reflects the encounter. The Pukhtuns say, "What we see in ourselves, we see in the world." Perhaps anthropologists would do well to keep the Pukhto proverb in mind.

Progress in the natural sciences often involves setting up experimental situations in the laboratory, and then seeing whether what happens confirms or disproves hypotheses previously formulated. Social scientists cannot usually test their hypotheses about human institutions in quite this way.

1. Some colonial anthropologists used — or misused — their position to conduct fieldwork. Nadel apparently employed a police squad to round up natives whenever he required respondents (Faris 1973).

28

Their laboratory is society itself, and where a researcher is dealing with human beings, other considerations besides the desire for knowledge, such as the subject's general well-being, legal and moral standards, and the national interest must have primacy. For this reason it is rarely feasible in social science to set up experimental situations on the natural science model. It is even less feasible to arrange that such situations are repeated under conditions which are for all practical purposes identical, as natural scientists do. The human experience is unique and not transferable to the chemist's experimental laboratory.

Social anthropologists must test their hypotheses about social and cultural institutions and their interconnections in the course of fieldwork in societies and situations which they have no power to control. Their tools are observation, interpretation, and comparison rather than experiment. This does not mean that anthropologists can do without theory. It is as essential to anthropology as it is to other scientific disciplines.

Whether we like it or not, social anthropology has become a specialist subject. It has its own theoretical equipment, some account of which has been given in preceding sections, and it has by now a considerable body of comparative material to draw upon. No one who writes about the social institutions of a small-scale community without knowledge of contemporary theory in social anthropology, and without some knowledge of the social and cultural institutions of comparable societies elsewhere, can hope to produce a scientifically adequate account. Without specialist training he cannot know the most important things to look for, the most useful questions to ask, or the best techniques for obtaining answers. In Victorian times there was no such body of sociological theory and comparative ethnography, and there was hardly any difference between the professional and the amateur. Today anyone who wishes to contribute significantly to the growing body of knowledge about the social and cultural institutions of small-scale and unfamiliar communities must acquire some theoretical training in social anthropology. At this preliminary stage, if the community and its culture differ greatly from his own, the anthropologist feels utterly bewildered and confused. The experience is a daunting one, and it can last for a long time. Most anthropologists have known the feelings of frustration and despondency — even of desperation — which go with the early stages of fieldwork in an unfamiliar culture. Anthropologists describe fieldwork as "an extremely personal traumatic kind of experience" (Leach 1971:91) which can be "painful and humiliating" (Wax 1971:19), and which can influence their work (Winter 1973:171).

Slowly, often imperceptibly, the early period passes. Living in a hut or tent within the village, the anthropologist gradually begins to understand what is happening around him. As his knowledge of the language and his acquaintance with the community advance, things begin to make sense. An overheard conversation is understood; a pattern of behavior is fitted to a learned social relationship. With luck he now has a few friends in the community, people who are willing to take time and trouble to explain things to him, to take him around the neighborhood and to introduce him to others. From this point onward, the pace accelerates. The anthropologist gets to know most of the members of the community as separate individuals, differing in temperament and in social status (and in their degree of interest in his work). He learns their often intricate ties of kinship and marriage; he comes to understand what they think about one another, about the world they live in, and about him. He learns not only what are the appropriate questions to ask, but of whom to ask them. He begins to feel "at home" in the community. He now knows it in some respect more thoroughly than he has ever known any community, even the one he grew up in. He has made the breakthrough into another culture: as a field anthropologist, he has arrived. He has accomplished the major characteristic of anthropological "participant observation".

To a Western anthropologist, probably born and brought up in an urban culture, this can be a vivid, almost traumatic, experience. The fieldworker who spends a year or more of his life as a member of a group of hunters and gatherers in Borneo, or of a tribe of African peasants or pastoralists, lives in more intimate contact with the basic conditions of human existence than has been possible for generations in the modern world. Birth, illness, and death, the daily effort to win food from the environment with the simplest equipment, the smell of the hot earth, the wind and the rain, the urgent, first-hand awareness of these things is something new and yet familiar to the visitor from a city culture. It is easy for anthropologists who have worked among such peoples to romanticise their experience and many do. The experience is an unforgettable one. The ideal social anthropological fieldworker is adaptable, tactful, good humored, and possessed of a sense of perspective. Above all, he is patient and considerate. He is, after all, a guest (though usually an uninvited one) in the community he is studying, and he must show the same respect and courtesy to his hosts as he expects to receive from them.

This is not the place for a detailed discussion of the various mechanical aids to field ethnography. Sound recording and photography may provide valuable supplements to the written record, and air photography can save weeks of labor where such matters as the dispersal of agricultural plots or patterns of village settlement are important. Mechanical aids, however, are not a substitute for the long and sustained personal contact upon which any comprehensive understanding of the community and its social and cultural life must be based.

The intensiveness of modern fieldwork, and the social anthropologist's increasing specialization, imply that he must become more and more dependent on other workers. In the communities which he studies, there are nearly always a few people who can read and write, and most fieldworkers engage one or two assistants, sometimes more, and pay them salaries. These assistants may not only serve as permanent informants and advisers; often they can make useful local contacts as well as collecting information and carrying out surveys under the anthropologist's supervision. The social anthropologist must participate as fully as he can in the everyday life of the community he is studying; he must live in it and get to know its members as people, as nearly as possible on equal terms. Evans-Pritchard claims that when he was studying divination among the Azande of the Sudan, he found it expedient to order his daily affairs by constant reference to the oracles, as the Azande do. He found this a more satisfactory way of making decisions than might be imagined.

No foreign anthropologist can ever be wholly assimilated to another culture; he can never quite become one with and indistinguishable from the people he is studying. Nor is it desirable that he should. "Stranger value" is an important asset. People often talk more freely to an outsider, so long as he is not too much of an outsider. Also, in a society where there are distinct social groups or classes, and especially when these are hierarchically arranged in terms of power and prestige, too close identification with one group or class may make easy contact with others difficult or impossible. This problem is particularly acute when societies like the caste communities of India are being studied, but it also arises in countries like Bunyoro and others in East Africa and elsewhere, where there is a marked difference between an aristocratic ruling class and the peasant population. One has to start one's intensive research at one level, and this may make it difficult later to achieve entry into the other. Plainly a great deal depends on the personality and temperament of the investigator.

III. THEORETICAL FRAMES IN WESTERN ANTHROPOLOGY

If it is virtually nonexistent in the Muslim world, anthropology in the West is in a state of general theoretical stagnation. Alarmist titles such as "Crisis of British Anthropology" (Banaji 1970) and "The Future of Social Anthropology: Disintegration or Metamorphosis?" (Needham 1970) reflect this. Apart from extending or varying the classical theoretical themes, contemporary anthropology has produced no major recent work. In addition, an acute sense of crisis accentuated by real problems — the shrinking job market, disappearing "primitive" groups, the emergence of "native anthropologists" — troubles the discipline. In particular the confidence of Western anthropology appears to be shaken by the emergence of the "native anthropologist". A leading Western anthropologist of Columbia University notes, "Akbar Ahmed's critique (1976) is also launched, although in a different sense, from within, since he represents one of those specters that haunts the anthropologist, a native of the society being studied" (Vincent 1978:185). Following is a brief summary of the major theoretical framework of Western anthropology.

It may be said that the anthropologist's first task is descriptive. In any empirical inquiry, we must know what the facts are before we can analyze them. Although the distinction between description and analysis is indispensable, it can be misleading, especially in the social sciences. The difference is not simply between studies which imply abstraction and those which do not. Even the most minimal descriptions include abstractions, generally unanalysed and implicit. This is because descriptions tend to be in general terms, and general terms are the names of classes, that is, of abstractions, and not the names of things. Description does more than describe, it also explains. Theories are involved in even the simplest descriptions. Not only do they determine the kinds of facts which are selected for attention, but also they dictate the ways in which these facts shall be ordered and put together. The important question is not whether an account of a social institution (or of anything else) implies generalization and abstraction, for this it does. The critical questions are: What is the level of abstraction, and what are the kinds of theories involved? It is especially necessary to be explicit in social anthropology, for the social situations it deals with are often unfamiliar ones. Anthropologists have thus devised different models to explain society which combine theory and empirical inquiry.

Thus the American anthropologist, Robert Redfield, developed the idea of the "folk" culture, and the French social anthropologist, Claude Lévi-Strauss, has distinguished the "statistical model" (the analyst's representation of the system being described) from the "mechanical model", the same system as its participant members regard it.

Lévi-Strauss's use of the term "statistical" is significant. "What actually happens" is susceptible to quantitative treatment in a way in which data of other kinds, such as beliefs and values, are not. Modern social anthropologists are required to do more than merely describe people's behavior qualitatively; they are also expected to support their assertions about what people do (or say they do) with some quantitative evidence. It is one thing to say, "such-and-such a people have the institution of bridewealth, whereby cattle and other goods pass from the bridegroom to the bride's family on marriage". It is quite another thing to say that "in 250 marriages, bridewealth was paid in 72 per cent of the sample". The latter statement really gives us "the facts".

The main focus of inquiry remains the social structure of the group.

A. Social Structure

Until very recently most social anthropologists, especially in Britain, have stressed the analysis of social systems as systems of action, that is, in causal terms. The most celebrated contributions of the past half-century (derived through Radcliffe-Brown and Malinowski from Durkheim and his predecessors) have been made at this level. The key which opened the door to the systematic understanding of the simpler, "primitive" societies was the organic analogy, which derived from French sociology. And the functioning of organisms, like the working of machines, makes sense without any reference to the states of mind of their constituent parts. Scholars on the

Continent and in America, and a few social anthropologists in Britain, have throughout sustained an interest in people's thoughts and ideas, both on their own account and as effective elements in systems of action. The theoretical models most characteristic of modern social anthropology have been those which take societies as systems of action, and which either explicitly or implicitly invoke the organic analogy. It is only in the last few years that the study of social and cultural institutions as systems of meanings has become of primary concern.

On the "action" level, two different though associated kinds of questions can be asked about social institutions, both concerned with causes. The first relates to the problem of how things came to be as they are, and so is essentially historical. A certain existing state of affairs is better understood if it can be shown to have followed from some pre-existing state of affairs in accordance with principles of causation already familiar from other contexts. If it can be shown (as it very often cannot) that a certain social institution is as it is because of certain historical happenings, social anthropologists take (or should take) note of these happenings, provided that there is sufficient evidence for them. The happenings need not themselves be physical events on the "action" plane of social reality; we know that ideas and values may play an important part in history. The second relates to the anthropologist's understanding of the current working of social attitudes and relations. History is not only important for sociology as a chain of causes and effects running back into the past. It is also important as a body of contemporary beliefs about those events. Such beliefs may be potent forces in current social attitudes and relations, and as such they are plainly the social anthropologist's concern.

The two most celebrated protagonists of functionalism in British social anthropology have been Malinowski and Radcliffe-Brown, and both of them claimed that their particular viewpoints provided a key to the understanding of societies and cultures as wholes, as well as to the understanding of particular institutions. Malinowski held that human society and culture are best understood as an assemblage of contrivances for satisfying the biological and psychological needs of the human organisms which make up the society. He found it necessary to supplement his list of needs with "derived" and "integrative" needs (not themselves strictly biological), but his central thesis was that anthropologists may best study human cultures as machines for satisfying men's organic needs.

Although the classification of human institutions in terms of the needs they serve (such as the provision of food, the propagation of the species, and the maintenance of physical security) provides convenient categories for fieldworkers to use, few if any anthropologists today find this approach satisfactory. Basic physical needs must be at least partly satisfied if human beings are to survive, and there can be no society without people. It is not illuminating to analyze social institutions solely in terms of such needs. Their satisfaction is a condition of the maintenance of any life, not only of social life, so they can hardly throw any distinctive light on the latter. The sociologist is interested in the conditions of living together, not merely of living. Since fundamental human needs are presumably much the same everywhere, differences between social and cultural institutions can never be explained by them. Every society has to provide for mating and reproduction, but if we want to know why some societies are monogamous and others polygamous, we shall have to seek our explanation in terms other than biological ones. Although Malinowski's contribution to modern social anthropology has been immense, his theoretical approach is not held in much regard today.

The second type of "total" functionalism, which Radcliffe-Brown derived largely from Durkheim, has been more influential. It asserts that the function of any social institution is the correspondence between it and some general need or, in Radcliffe-Brown's phrase, some "necessary condition of existence" of the society. Radcliffe-Brown wrote of society as if it were some kind of real existence, and he thought that the ultimate value for any society is its continued survival. This, so his argument goes, can only be achieved through the maintenance of social solidarity or cohesion between its members. They must tolerate, respect and cooperate with one another, to a sufficient degree. Social solidarity is the end to which social institutions must contribute, and this contribution is their function. Radcliffe-Brown does say that functionalism is a hypothesis, not a dogma; his thesis is that social institutions may contribute to the maintenance of the whole society. He does not claim that they must invariably do so. Thus in his first and most celebrated book, *The Andaman Islanders,* he gives a functional explanation of certain of the ritual institutions of this preliterate and technologically simple people. What he does is show that their rites express symbolically, and so help to sustain, certain social attitudes and values which are conducive to the smooth running of community life. Radcliffe-Brown thought of social function in the context of what he sometimes called "the total social system", and he asserted that functional unity is achieved when "all parts of the social system work together with a sufficient degree of harmony or internal consistency; that is without producing persistent conflicts which can neither be resolved nor regulated."

The first thing to observe is how heavily this formulation depends on the organic analogy; it seems to imply that a "total social system" is an empirical entity to which definite attributes can be ascribed. Radcliffe-Brown is still tacitly assuming that a society is something very like an organism, although this view seems no longer tenable. In recent years, it has become clear that the "holistic" view of society that it implies is of little value in actual research. How, for example, could the lack of "a sufficient degree of harmony" be proved except by the physical destruction of the whole community? In any case "society" is not something given in experience. It is an intellectual construct or model, built up on the basis of experience, but not itself a datum. Society is a way of ordering experience, a working and for certain purposes indispensable hypothesis. If we impute substantial reality to it, we saddle ourselves with an entity which is more embarrassing than useful.

A functional explanation which refers to society or societies as existent wholes, has little practical value for social anthropologists. On the other hand the sociological functionalism of the 20's and 30's has added greatly to our knowledge by showing how social institutions may be interdependent with other institutions and how they "fit together" in various institutional complexes, such as political, economic, or ritual systems.

The organic analogy has led to error in one further respect. It implies not only that societies are empirically given systems, but also that they are harmoniously integrated ones, or should be if they are "healthy". These systems are then thought of as being in a state of equilibrium or "homeostasis" by a set of smoothly interacting and somehow self-adjusting social institutions.

To summarize, the notions of social function and social structure have been the most important forces in British social anthropology during the past half-century. By the study of social function, anthropologists have generally meant the study of the causal implications of social institutions for other social institutions and systems of institutions in the same society. By the study of social structure they have generally meant the definition of those enduring aspects of social institutions which have appeared to be most important in terms of their interest in them. Modern British social anthropology has sometimes been identified with what has been called the "structural-functional approach". Although there is much more to British social anthropology than this, these concepts have provided the operational framework for many field studies of high quality.

The structural-functional model derives much of its effectiveness from the analogy with organic systems, which can be regarded as complex wholes whose parts work together to ensure the harmonious functioning of the whole system. Though the analogy has proved useful, it has serious limitations when applied to communities of human beings, who differ from the mindless components of natural or mechanical systems in being themselves conscious, willing agents sharing with the social scientists who study them the power of conceptual thinking, representing their social and material universe to themselves, and acting in accordance with these representations. The structural-functional approach sometimes took insufficient account of this fact, although its practitioners have recognized that people's ideas may be causally effective. If a human community is regarded primarily in its dimension as a system of action rather than as a system of ideas and symbols, then the distinction between the analytical system and the "folk" system is unlikely to command much attention, any more than it does in the study of other causal systems, like biological or mechanical ones.

It may be said that despite the great advances in our understanding of the working of small-scale societies as revealed by the development of functional and structural theory, this development has tended to distract attention from the equally important problem of how to understand other

35

peoples' systems of beliefs and values. Systems of beliefs and values were of interest to anthropologists long before the intensive development of structural-functional theory, but it is only quite recently that the interests of a significant number of British anthropologists have returned to them. There has been a tendency to regard ideas and values as "cultural" data, and for many years "culture" has been regarded at best as a peripheral interest of structurally oriented social anthropologists. It is now more generally recognized that the social anthropologist is directly and legitimately concerned with both dimensions.

A larger argument envelops and partly overlaps these schools. I refer to Marxist anthropology. Anthropologists calling themselves Marxist employ traditional Marxist tools to analyze social structure, organization and relationships. Talal Asad's analysis of the Swat Pukhtuns, for example, is a straightforward and successful class analysis[1] (Asad 1972). The usefulness of Marxist theory is somewhat curtailed in the overenthusiasm of Marxist scholars wishing to apply their theoretical framework irrespective of ecology or ethnography. For instance Marxist analyses of segmentary societies living in low production zones (Rey 1975, Terray 1972, 1975 a and b) remain unsatisfactory and have been termed by Godelier, himself a Marxist, "vulgar Marxisms" (Godelier 1977).

B. Kinship and Political Organization

According to the dictionary, kinship has to do with relationships by blood, or consanguinity, whereas affinity has to do with relationships brought about by marriage. In social anthropology the two topics are very closely connected. All cultures distinguish various categories of kin and affines, and these categories with their associated patterns of rights and obligations make up what social anthropologists call kinship systems. In some societies every individual is, or thinks he is, related by kinship or affinity to everyone else. In others, including most Western societies, a man's kin and affines are limited for practical purposes to a few close relatives. In every society, however, some relationships of kinship and affinity are culturally recognized.

Social anthropologists are accused of concerning themselves overmuch with the refinements and complexities of kinship terminologies, of indulging in what Malinowski called "kinship algebra", and there are good reasons for this concern. Very few of the interpersonal relationships which make up a Western European's social world are kinship ones. Kinship plays little or no part in his relations with his friends, his employers, his teachers, his colleagues, or in the complex network of political, economic and religious associations in which he is involved. But in many smaller-scale societies, kinship's social importance is paramount. Where a person lives, his group

1. For uneven Marxist analyses of Punjab villages see Ahmad, S 1977 and Alavi 1971, 1972.

and community membership, whom he should obey and by whom be obeyed, who his friends are and who his enemies are, whom he may and may not marry, from whom he may hope to inherit and to whom pass on his own status and property — all these matters and many more may be determined by his status in a kinship system. Where everyone is or thinks of himself as being related to nearly everyone else, almost all social relationships must be kinship or affinal ones too. Even in societies where kinship is less pervasive, it usually plays a much more important part than it does in modern urban and industrialised Western societies.

Why is kinship so important in small-scale societies? The short answer is that in all human communities, even the most technologically simple ones, the basic categories of biological relationship are available as a means of identifying and ordering social relations. This is true even though some of these categories may be differently defined in different cultures. Everywhere people are begotten of men and born of women, and in most societies the fact of parenthood and the bonds of mutual dependency and support that it implies are acknowledged. It also leads to the recognition of other links, such as those between siblings (children of the same parents), and between grandparents and their grandchildren. Even in the simplest societies, kinship provides some ready-made categories for distinguishing between the people one is born among, and ordering one's relations with them. Apart from sex and age, which are also of prime social importance, there is no other way of classifying people which is so "built-in" to the human condition.

From a biological point of view not only human beings but all animals have "kinship". The vital point is that, unlike other animals, human beings consciously and explicitly use the categories of kinship to define social relationships. When an anthropologist speaks of a parent-child relationship, or of the relationship between cross-cousins (the children of a brother and a sister), he is not primarily concerned with the biological connections between these kinds of kin, although he recognizes the existence of such relations. What he is concerned with are the social relationships between kin and the fact that in the culture being studied, kinship involves distinct types of social behaviour, and particular patterns of expectations, beliefs and values. Kinship is especially relevant in tribal society.

Radcliffe-Brown's formulation, based on the classical definitions used by Max Weber and others, is more useful, though we shall see that it is not quite adequate either. In the Preface to *African Political Systems* he wrote that political organization is concerned with "the maintenance or establishment of social order, within a territorial framework, by the organised exercise of coercive authority through the use, or the possibility of use, of physical force." This definition employs two different criteria. First, reference is made to the end to which political activity is directed, and regulation and control of the social order within a certain territory. And secondly, the means whereby this is achieved is brought in, the organized exercise of authority backed by force. Social anthropologists can make good use of the first of these criteria. For some degree of social order is attained in every society, and social anthropologists are interested in finding out how this is done. They are concerned in identifying and analyzing the social institutions through which order is maintained on a territorial or tribal basis and through which relationships with other territorial or tribal groups are created and maintained. It is not disconcerting that some institutions, like the blood feud in certain societies, are not what we ordinarily think of as "political". Our interest is in the realities of social life, not primarily in the names we use to identify these realities. We do, however, have to use words with care, lest the reality be obscured. When we are discussing political phenomena in small-scale societies, there is much to be said for speaking of the political aspect of certain social institutions, rather than of specifically political institutions. Often institutions which have political importance are socially significant in a number of other contexts as well.

The second of Radcliffe-Brown's criteria, the organized exercise of authority backed by force, leads to difficulty when it is applied to some of the societies which anthropologists study. Anthropologists can certainly speak of authority and force when they are considering centralised states like those with which most of us are familiar in the Western world, with their kings, parliaments, courts, judges and police forces. Many of the smaller-scale societies are of this type, though usually their political organisation is less elaborate. But some of them are not. In such tribes as the Nuer, or the Tallensi of northern Ghana, there are (or were) no specialised political functionaries, and there is no organised structure of authority backed by physical force. (This is not to say that physical force is not exercised in such societies.) Nonetheless, these societies do possess order and structural continuity; they may even be shown to have a political structure. The fact that political authority may be widely diffused, for example, among grades of elders or lineage heads, and that it may be backed by religious or magical sanctions rather than by organised physical force, does not mean that such authority is lacking, though it may be relatively unspecialised and very hard to identify.

Even where no political authorities at all can be found, as in some segmentary societies, the ends, which I have defined as political, may be brought about through the interplay of other institutions not overtly political. We shall see later how this happens. Here, as elsewhere, the classical conceptual apparatus of Western culture does not quite fit much of the unfamiliar social material.

To the question, how political order is thought of and maintained (so far as it is maintained) in segmentary, lineage-based societies where there are no political authorities to make and enforce political decisions, there is no short and simple answer. The maintenance of some degree of territorial order is a function of several different social institutions. Where lineal descent provides the principle upon which corporate local groups are established, it provides also the idiom through which inter-group, even inter-tribal, relations operate, as we saw in the case of the blood

38

feud. Where, as among the Nuer, lineal membership or nonmembership is a relevant aspect of practically all social relationships, then lineal attachments and loyalties provide a framework for territorial relations also, and territorial grouping and lineal structure tend to show a rough-and-ready correlation. Even where other factors besides lineal membership play a significant part in many social situations, as among the Tallensi, the lineal organisation is still of great importance. Once again, the matter is very much one of degree. The question is not so much whether such and such people "have" lineages. The important questions are these: What kind of social and political importance, if any, does lineal descent have in the society concerned? If groups are formed on this basis, how large are they and of how many generations do they take account? What patterns of social behavior and value are associated with membership in these groups?

The role of lineal descent as an organizational principle varies widely in different societies but it is generally agreed that there are certain broad categories of rights and obligations which attach to and are transmitted by descent. In many societies these broad categories relate to jural, social, and political status in the widest sense, and are applicable by definition to those groups who have a place on the genealogical charter. Although segmentary societies possess unusual diffusion of power and tendency to egalitarianism among collaterals, the democracy is structural rather than ideological and there are no political theories or written principles to support it.

Lineal descent and the accompanying social behaviour implies and imposes through the social Code, acts as an indicator distinguishing those on the genealogical charter from those not on it. There is thus an exaggerated social awareness of lineal descent in many societies. Ideally identical segments are arranged symmetrically on the genealogical chart and the ascendant or descendant levels structurally reflect one another. Segmentary structure and the principle of lineal descent pervade the whole system and contribute to social cohesion. The political superstructure of segmentary tribes tracing descent from a common apical ancestor is an extension of this segmentary lineal organisation. The descent chart defines a hierarchy of homologous groups which can direct fusion or fission of social and political interests within a merging or diverging series of such groups. Ideally such tribal genealogy "is a conceptualisation of a hierarchy of ordered territorial segments" (Peters, 1960:31). In such societies at every level, a high degree of consistency between ecological divisions and genealogical divisions is apparent.

When we turn to consider "centralized" societies, we are faced with similar problems of identification and of degree. As Lucy Mair has recently pointed out, we cannot simply divide societies into those which have chiefs and those which don't. If we could, the classification of small-scale political systems would be much simpler. Two factors contribute to the difficulty of classification. The first is that lineal organization may still be of major political importance even in societies which have a titular head or king, and which may therefore be characterised as centralized. If, for example, the

39

segmentary Nuer were to acknowledge one man, or one lineage, as ritually pre-eminent, while retaining their present segmentary social organization, should we say that they had a centralised political system? We would, rightly, hesitate to do so, and yet a common loyalty to a central head, however tenuous and however restricted the authority allotted to him, certainly has political implications. When we are considering so-called centralised societies, we have to look very closely at the nature and scope of the political authority (if there is any), which is centralised in such societies.

The second, more taxonomic factor was touched on earlier. It is that there are many societies or social aggregates, possessing a common language and culture and more or less conscious of their tribal identity, which have no central head, but which consist of congeries of small, relatively independent units. These units may be based neither on lineal kin groups nor on age sets. They may themselves be politically centralised statelets or chiefdoms, each centered on its own chief and politically independent of all the others. The important Sukuma and Nyamwezi peoples of Tanzania form such groups. Whether we regard them as centralised or as segmentary societies depends upon whether we regard them from the point of view of their component units, or from the point of view of the whole social aggregate. On the whole it is most useful to speak of such societies as centralised, for unlike the strictly segmentary societies discussed in the first part of this section, their members do look to an individual head. His significance may be either ritual, or political, or both, but his primacy is acknowledged over a wider social field than family or village. We shall do well to bear in mind, first, that centralisation is very much a matter of degree, and of the point of view from which the social situation is regarded, and second, that centralisation, however we define it, is only one of a number of criteria which it is useful to employ in classifying small-scale social systems.

Even though kings of this kind lack political authority, they are usually regarded with veneration, even awe. Often such a king is symbolically identified with his whole country, and it is believed that any physical injury to him must damage the country as a whole. So he has to maintain full physical vigor for as long as he reigns. If he begins to fail, it is believed that he may be (or may have been in the past) secretly killed by his wives or ministers, so that the country he reigns over shall not share in his decline. Frazer's well-known account of divine kingship refers to this symbolic kind of king. The point is not that the king is actually thought of as specially near to God or the gods and so may intercede with them on his people's behalf (though this too is sometimes the case). It is rather that he is seen as somehow above and different from ordinary people, for in a sense he not only represents but is the whole country. So he is thought to possess a unique prestige and virtue.

The classical example of such a king is the Reth of the Shilluk of the Upper Nile, of whom Evans-Pritchard has written that he "reigns but does not govern". The Shilluk people are organised in agnatic lineages similar in many respects to those of the Nuer, and order is maintained through "self-help" rather than by means of any kind of centralised administration. Even though his political role is minimal or even non-existent, the king in societies of this kind still has political importance, as he is a visible expression of the unity of the people he reigns over, and their identification with him distinguishes them from other neighboring peoples. It may also happen, as indeed it has happened in the case of the Shilluk, that a kingship whose primary function is symbolic, and which is traditionally associated with little or no political power, may become invested with such power in consequence of social change and the impact of foreign rule. For example, the availability of guns may enable a particular individual (and so his whole line if his office is hereditary) to establish a political as opposed to a merely ritual dominance, for which there is no traditional warrant. Also, an imposed European administration may unknowingly endow, with the power to make political decisions, persons who had formerly no right to do so.

In conclusion, *African Political Systems* (Fortes and Evans-Pritchard, 1970) distinguishes three types of tribal social organisation: the Bushmen, where political relations equal kin relations (*ibid:* 6-7); the second type, called Group A, are unitary states with kings or paramount chiefs ruling centralised states with societies that are ranked; the third type, Group B, are segmentary lineage systems, characterized by: (1) Segmentation of tribal groups; (2) Lineal descent from a common eponymous ancestor (Patrilineal descent is of primary importance as against matrilineal descent in other societies), (Leach, 1971b); (3) Monadism wherein "the small group is the embryo tribe, and the tribe is the smaller group writ large" (Gellner, 1969:48); and finally, (4) Egalitarianism or an acephalous form of political organisation. To these categories of tribal systems may be added another classification, that of the "segmentary state" (Southall, 1953).

C. Beliefs, Magic and Religion

Social anthropologists have always had to take some account of the beliefs and values of the peoples they study. Although functional theory has tended to distract attention from this field, it has greatly advanced our understanding of other people's ways of thought. It has done so mainly because of its emphasis on fieldwork. This understanding implies reference to what people think, as no human social institutions or relationships can be adequately understood unless account is taken of the expectations, beliefs and values which they involve. Nevertheless, with a few notable exceptions, systematic field studies of people's modes of thought, their values and beliefs, have only recently begun to be made.

For the earlier anthropologists, problems about the modes of thought of so-called "primitives" scarcely arose with any complexity. It was easy for the Victorians to assume that such thinking as primitives did was simple and "childish" (one of their favorite adjectives), an inferior version of their own. The intensive fieldwork which was to provide an intimate understanding of "simpler" people's way of life and thought, and so to demonstrate the superficiality and inadequacy of such views, had not begun.

In France, in the early years of this century, the famous sociologist, Emile Durkheim, founded a school of social anthropologists which was called the *Année Sociologique* group, after the journal they founded. These writers devoted much attention to the study of the ideas, their *représentations collectives*, which so-called "primitive" peoples held about themselves and about the world around them. Like their predecessors, these scholars did little or no fieldwork, so they were dependent for their information mostly on the reports of travelers and missionaries, which varied a good deal in quality.

I want to stress that it was only with the development of intensive fieldwork that the subtlety, complexity and, often, profundity of the ways of thought of preliterate or only recently literate peoples began to be at all adequately understood. As soon as anthropologists began to live for periods of months and even years among the people they studied, communicating with them in their own tongue and sharing in their daily activities, it began to become plain that the old Western stereotypes about primitive modes of thought were quite inadequate, and often misleading. A landmark in the growth of this recognition is Evans-Pritchard's *Witchcraft, Oracles and Magic among the Azande (1937)*. In this study the beliefs of this highly intelligent people of the southern Sudan are shown, not as a set of weird and irrational delusions about occult forces, but rather as embodying a mode of adjustment to the strains and frustrations of everyday life, which in the whole context of Zande culture is eminently practical and sensible. The Zande system of beliefs, and others like it, provide both an explanation of misfortune (Why did this have to happen to me?) and a way of dealing with it. In a pre-scientific culture there may be no other means of coping with such situations.

Let me briefly refer to Radcliffe-Brown's theory of ritual. His argument states that one of the functions of ritual is to express and so to reinforce certain sentiments or value adherance to which the smooth running of the society depends. The important truth which this view contains is now plain. Ritual, magic, and taboo, are essentially symbolic and so expressive, and they are often thought to be instrumental as well. Certainly they may have important social consequences for the people who have them. The difficulty with Radcliffe-Brown's account of ritual, is that it is too general to be of much practical use in investigating real human cultures. To say, as he does, that the communal performance of ritual may express, and so sustain, values which contribute to the maintenance of social solidarity may be true. But it is not always so. Communal ritual may be divisive as well as cohesive, and notions other than social solidarity may be symbolically expressed by it. Some of the rites involved in sorcery, for example, can hardly be said to sustain patterns of behaviour which are conducive to social cohesion. Further, Radcliffe-Brown's hypothesis, as he states it, affords no room for testing. Social cohesion itself is taken to be exhibited by the communal

42

performances which are supposed to sustain it. There is circularity in the argument that dancing together contributes to the kind of situation in which people like to dance together. The thesis could only be disproved by finding a society which failed to carry out the necessary ritual and therefore perished. To Radcliffe-Brown's great merit, however (following Durkheim), he made the point that ritual is an essentially expressive activity, and that it can and does have important social implications. Society is the indispensable condition of human life as we know it, and in worshipping God man is really worshipping his own social system.

Durkheim's theory of religion has been subjected to a good deal of criticism. It is rather less naive than it appears to be, when we realise (and Durkheim sometimes failed to make this clear) that society is not a "thing", but rather a system of relationships, in some sense a construct. Social relationships, involving beliefs, expectations, and values as well as human interactions in space and time, are not "given" empirically, in the same sense that the data of the natural sciences are. It is one thing to say that totemism, or religion, means that a man worships the actual group of people of which he is a member. It is quite a different thing to say that what he is revering is a complex system of moral imperatives, of rights and obligations, the observance of which is a condition of ordered social life. It was the latter that Durkheim meant, not the former, though sometimes he was less than clear on this point. What he did was to raise to the level of a sociological principle, the Christian maxim that all men are members one of another. Most modern students of religion would hold, as against Durkheim, that religious belief and practice are more than merely a system of social and moral symbolism. Group symbolism can be very important, in secular as well as in religious contexts, and it was to Durkheim's great merit that he pointed this out.

As a theory of totemism, it is not quite adequate, although it makes the important point that totems, like flags and old school ties in Western societies, are symbols of group unity. It is worth mentioning in passing what the great psychologist, Sigmund Freud, contributed to the study of totemism. Like Durkheim, he based his hypothesis on the Australian material. He surmised that the origin of the institution lay in the Oedipus complex, which he held to be universal. In the primeval family, he said, the sons covet their father's wives, and in order to acquire them they kill and eat their father. Afterwards they are smitten with remorse, and the totemic feast (which occurred in Australia but is found nowhere else) is really a symbolic re-enacting of that first patricidal crime. Freud does not make clear at what point in human history he thinks that this happened, or whether it happened only once or on many occasions. His theory is not taken seriously by social anthropologists, who in any case are not greatly interested in the undiscoverable origins of human institutions. What Freud does is to translate what is undoubtedly a scientific insight of profound importance (at least in Western cultures) from psychological into socio-historical terms. But, this turns it into an undemonstrable and therefore valueless hypothesis, significant only as a mythical expression of psycho-analytic values (Freud 1950).

The term totemism covers a multitude of phenomena. As it is generally used, however, it refers to situations where each one of a number of discrete social groups into which a society is divided maintains a particular regard — though not necessarily one of worship or reverence — for a particular object in the natural or cultural spheres.

This leads to a final point. What is symbolised in religious behavior? Durkheim said that in totemism (for him the elementary form of religion) society is worshipping itself, or to put it more sophisticatedly, men are asserting and so reinforcing the importance of the system of mutual interdependencies which constitute society. Radcliffe-Brown argued that ritual expresses symbolically certain sentiments or values, upon the acceptance of which the smooth running of society itself depends. This view is essentially a restatement of Durkheim's position, and like it, it obscures the important fact that conflict and opposition may be important components of social systems as well as harmony, and may also become focuses of ritual. Radcliffe-Brown argued also that ritual sometimes expresses more than man's need of society, it expresses his fundamental dependence on the natural world which he occupies and of which he is a part.

We have seen that much ritual and religious behavior translates uncontrollable natural forces into symbolic entities which, through the performance of ritual, can be manipulated and dealt with. Ritual is a language for saying things which are felt to be true and important but which are not susceptible to statement in scientific terms. Even if sophisticated modern man is less inclined to attach instrumental efficacy to the symbols which he has created to express his apprehension of the universe and of its ultimate meaning, he still feels the need to express this awareness. In the areas beyond science, there is no way of expressing it except symbolically. To say that religious symbols are man-made is not to decry the validity of religion, for ritual is a statement about something, not just about itself. But the comparative study of the religious beliefs and practices of other cultures may suggest that in religion, no less than in other forms of symbolic behavior, reality is misrepresented if the symbol, and not the often indefinable thing that it symbolises, is taken to be the ultimate truth.

D. Economic Anthropology

This section may be introduced by briefly mentioning the two main theoretical positions in economic anthropology, Substantivist versus Formalist. Polanyi (1968b:122) sums up the respective positions thus: The Substantivist economic approach (1) derives from fact, (2) implies neither choice nor insufficiency of means, (3) implies power of gravity, and (4) laws of nature (Bohannan, P. 1959; Bohannan, P. and L., 1968; Bohannan and Dalton, 1962; Dalton, 1961, 1962, 1965, 1967, 1968, 1969; Meillasoux, 1964,

44

1972; Polanyi, 1944, 1966, 1968 a and b; Polanyi *et al.*, 1957; Sahlins, 1968, 1969). The Formalist approach (1) derives from logic, (2) has sets of rules referring to choices between alternative uses of insufficient means, (3) has the power of syllogism, and (4) derives from the laws of the mind (Burling, 1962; Cancian, 1966; Deane, 1953, Epstein, 1962; Firth, 1964, 1966, 1970; Hill, 1963, 1965; LeClair, 1962; Salisbury, 1962). The title of Cancian's paper "Maximisation as Norm, Strategy and Theory" (1966) clearly states the Formalist position. Volumes containing both viewpoints are standard academic fare (Firth, 1970; LeClair and Schneider 1968).

Without wishing to become involved in a Substantivist versus Formalist debate in economic anthropology on which there is a flourishing and sophisticated literature, few anthropologists or economists would deny that there exists the closest possible relationship between social groups and their economic environment and those activities which determine social organisation in society.

The study of the economics of simpler societies falls into two main divisions, and I deal with these separately. First, there is the question how people manage to extract the physical necessities of life from their environment; here we are concerned with the means by which resources are exploited and the kinds of social activities involved in production. Second, there is the question, What is done with the goods after they are produced? In the end, of course, they are (mostly) consumed, but often quite complex mechanisms of distribution and exchange are involved, and not all of these can be understood simply in economic terms.

A first and most essential requirement for any human community is to feed itself, and in some of the very simple societies this is everybody's main preoccupation from childhood to death. It is a truism that everything we eat, whether animal, vegetable or (occasionally) mineral, comes either directly or indirectly from the earth. This is much less obvious to the modern man who lives in a world of processed foods and supermarkets, than it is to a member of a peasant community, living at or near a bare subsistence level. As well as food, the environment also produces shelter, clothing and essential tools. Anthropologists have usually distinguished three main methods by which these necessities have been secured, and in the eighteenth century and later it was usual to rank the communities which practised them in an evolutionary order of "progress". The very simplest communities subsist entirely by, as it were, raiding the environment; these are the hunters, collectors, and sometimes fishermen. They obtain their livelihood, often with remarkable ingenuity, by gathering wild fruit, roots and so on in season, and by hunting and trapping. The Eskimo are such a people, and have achieved a remarkable command over a very harsh environment. Tropical forest peoples like the pygmies of equatorial Africa and South East Asia have a far simpler technology, and a less rigorous environment to cope with. Dwellers in arid regions like the territory of the South African bushmen and the Australian aborigines have developed delicate adjustments to their sparse environment. In consequence material goods are few and easily portable, and often there is no tribal organisation over and above the level of the small family groups which compose the effective economic units. It is natural that in such conditions the very highest value is usually attached to the solidarity of these small groups, for every one is dependent on the support and cooperation of his fellows.

At some time in the unrecorded past, men began to domesticate wild animals. With the domestication of such important species as cattle, goats and sheep it became possible for human communities to sustain life on the produce of their flocks and herds. Though many societies, including the most "advanced", have a mixed pastoral and agricultural economy, the emphasis differs widely from society to society, and there are still many people who subsist wholly, or almost wholly, on their herds. Some nomadic peoples of the Asian steppe fall, or fell, into this category, as do the Nilo-Hamitic Masai of East Africa. Traditionally the Masai lived exclusively on the meat, milk, and blood provided by their cattle; they rejected vegetable foods and despised those who dug the earth to produce them. This way of life also imposes certain restrictions on those who practice it. They must have adequate supplies of grazing and water for their stock, and often this means that they cannot stay for very long in the same place. Sometimes they are transhumant, which means that they make seasonal movements from their base in search of water and grass. Sometimes they are strictly nomadic, that is, they are forever on the move to new pastures. A pastoral way of life also imposes limits on possible population density; a herding population is more thinly scattered on the ground (though usually not so thinly as hunters and collectors), and this precludes intensive or highly centralised administration. It is often said of pastoral people that they are independent and resentful of authority. It is easy to see why this should be so. It is easy to see, too, why their social systems are so often adapted to raiding and warfare. Unlike some other forms of property, livestock are easily stolen and transported, and raiding is a common diversion in many such societies.

Agriculture makes possible a more settled way of life. Although in many parts of the world cultivation is of the shifting "slash and burn" type, whereby new ground is cleared for planting every few years and old gardens allowed to revert to bush, this mode of subsistence does permit long residence in the same area. It also entails a different attitude toward land from that commonly held by hunters and herders. Whatever the system of land holding, cultivators, as individuals, families, or lineages have a very specific, if rarely exclusive, concern with the plots of land they cultivate and from which they hope to harvest. This is not the place to discuss the growth of the first great civilisations that originated with the early cultivators in the great river valleys of the Middle East and elsewhere. Certain consequences of an agricultural way of life should be noted. First, the greater population density possible, combined with the relative stability of agricultural populations, enables the establishment of wider-scale political units than family or clan. In some fertile areas such as West Africa (to say nothing of the early riverine civilisations), agriculture has also made possible urban

46

concentrations of considerable size, with all the administrative complexity that this implies. Another consequence of the adoption of agriculture has been the emergence of a leisured class and, often, of some form of aristocracy. With good growing conditions and suitable crops, a cultivator, unlike a hunter or a herder, need not give all his time to food production. Also, a surplus may be produced which can be used to feed noncultivators, who may thus be freed for other forms of productive activity.

This type of analysis was first systematically undertaken by Durkheim in his famous book *The Division of Labour*. Characteristically, his primary concern was sociological rather than economic. He wanted to know just what were the forces which bind men together into communities; what were the bonds of social cohesion? He concluded that social cohesion could be sustained in two ways. The first is through what he called mechanical solidarity. This is a state of affairs in which all or most of the members of the cooperating group, be they hunters, herders, cultivators or something else, carry out the same kinds of tasks. Thus conformity to a common set of rules is the paramount value, and Durkheim thought that this conformity was achieved through the fear of punishment, either secular or supernatural. As we saw in the last chapter, Malinowski showed the inadequacy of this model if it be taken to represent the way in which any "primitive" society actually lives. In contrast to this kind of solidarity Durkheim proposed as a later and more civilised type of cooperation, what he called organic solidarity. Here the bounds lie not in conformity to rules (though of course there are rules and conformity is required), but rather in individual group specialisation, so that some people produce some kinds of goods or services, and other people other kinds. These are then reciprocally exchanged, so that, like the constituent members of an organism, every man is dependent on the activity of other men, their joint activities contributing to the smooth running of the whole community. Durkheim thought that in such a system, repressive sanctions tend to be replaced by restitutive ones; the fulfilment of contractual obligations and not conformity to rules is the cement which binds society together.

Polanyi (1968b) made his major contribution to economic anthropology by distinguishing three main categories of economic relationships in society: reciprocity, redistribution, and exchange. Reciprocity denotes movements between correlative points and symmetrical groupings, redistribution designates movements towards the center and out of it again, and exchange refers to vice versa movements taking place under a market system. Sahlins further analysed reciprocity (Sahlins, 1969). Although this theoretical categorisation of economic relationships within tribal structure is an interesting starting point for a discussion on economic interaction within tribal groups, I cannot sustain it with my own data. In its simple form reciprocity is a "between" relationship, the action and response of two parties, whereas redistribution is a "within" relationship, the collective action of a group with a defined socio-center where goods are concentrated and thence flow outward. "Redistribution is chieftainship said in economics" (Sahlins, 1968:95).

In this section I have attempted to illustrate the close relationship between forms of social organisation and economic environment. But society is rarely static. Let us turn to a discussion of the processes of social change.

E. Processes of Social Change

Change is taking place in all human societies all the time. Sometimes it is sudden and catastrophic, as when a system of government is destroyed by revolution and replaced by a radically different ruling system. Sometimes it is so gradual and imperceptible that even the members of the society themselves scarcely notice it. But, it is always there, and social anthropologists who wish to understand the working of the societies they study must take account of it. Here they must be the historian. Changes take place in time, and they can only be understood as causal sequences of events leading to new states of affairs. These new states of affairs are "the present", and that is what the social anthropologist is trying to understand. He is a historian, but only in a particular context and for a particular purpose.

Social change cannot be studied as though it were a separate social field, indistinguishable from the other topics which have been discussed in the preceding sections. The student of change is concerned with all aspects of inquiry. He can no more study "social" change in general than he can study "society" in general. His data are specific social and cultural institutions, and he has to study the modifications of these through time, in the context of co-existing social, cultural and, sometimes, ecological factors. One might wonder whether such study will reveal any general laws of social change, though certain trends, characteristic of certain conditions, times and places, may be detected. One such is considered below. For it is now evident that changes in people's social and cultural institutions through time are not to be understood in terms of any single "blanket" principle. A multiplicity of social processes is involved, and these often operate concurrently. One of these is conflict within society.

Though there is conflict in all societies, it may differ considerably in kind and degree. It is a sadly common observation of anthropologists (and others) that under the stress of culture contact many of the societies have ceased to function as they once did, and in some cases have broken down altogether. Sometimes social systems, even people, have been totally or almost destroyed. The Tasmanian aborigines, the Tierra del Fuegians, and the North American Indians are examples. Often the damage has been more subtle, though hardly less radical. The functional, organic model seemed plausible enough when it was applied to those small-scale societies which were virtually unaffected by outside contact, and which had apparently not changed significantly in generations. However, when increasing contact with the West brought radical social change and new and more disruptive

48

social conflicts, and when the more intensive fieldwork of modern times disclosed these changes and conflicts, then this approach, by itself, became plainly inadequate. There was no use plastering up the cracks in institutional functionalism with concepts like dysfunction (a notion better expressed by Durkheim in his concept of anomie or "lawlessness"; a state of affairs in which hitherto accepted and acceptable standards are no longer meaningful). The functional model still implied the untenable assumption that there was an ideally harmonious, "functional" state of society, and that this had somehow been breached.

Social anthropologists have increasingly concerned themselves with situations of conflict and social stress, and they have done so mostly in the context of culture contact. But "conflict" is a vague term. Two problems, in particular, arise. We must ask, first, What are the things that are supposed to be in conflict and second, What kind or degree of conflict is it that concerns us?

Anthropologists have accordingly distinguished between two kinds of social conflict, and so between two kinds of social change. First there are those conflicts and changes which are provided for in the existing social structure. The Nuer blood feud, or the succession struggles which occur in many states when the king dies, are examples of these. Obviously changes in personnel are a feature of every society, as all people grow old, die, and are replaced by others. But so long as the roles themselves continue more or less unchanged, these conflicts and replacements do not affect the structure of the social system itself. They operate within its existing framework, are resolvable in terms of shared systems of values, and offer no challenge to the existing institutions.

The second kind of change is more radical. It is change in the character of the social system itself: some of its constituent institutions are altered, so that they no longer "mesh" with other co-existing institutions as they once did. This is structural or "radical" change, and the conflicts to which it gives rise are not resolvable in terms of the existing values of the society. Structural changes engender new kinds of conflicts, and tradition provides neither precedents nor cures for them. They are especially disturbing, and involve confusion and strain. If the social system is to persist, sooner or later further radical modifications will have to be made in it, and so the society will become something other than what it originally was. Here again, the ineptness of the organic analogy for the understanding of social change may be noted: organisms do not change from one species into completely different ones. Under the stress of social change, societies often do.

To these two types of change Firth has added a third one that he calls organisational change. Organisational changes are changes in ways of doing things, which themselves continue to be done, and in the extent and range of particular complexes of social relationships, which remain formally unaltered. This further distinction is useful, although in the last resort, structure and organisation are rather two aspects of the same reality than two different things. Having stated the major positions of Western anthropology let me attempt to explain where and how Orientalist literature has influenced perception of Muslim societies.

IV. THE ORIENTALIST ANTHROPOLOGIST

Edward Said's *Orientalism* is a powerful indictment of the subject and its practitioners. He states explicitly the prejudices and tendentious arguments of the Orientalists. It is also altogether too passionate and angry an argument. Because of the power and passion, the more down-to-earth simpler weaknesses of Orientalist scholarship are left out. For instance, rather than accusing Bernard Lewis of mental exhaustion, moral bankruptcy etc. I would have, as an anthropologist, pointed out some of the conceptual weaknesses in his study. His categories of tribe and peasant in society are seriously at fault (Lewis 1966). The one is often employed for the other. This to an anthropologist is not a minor slip.

My quarrel is with some of the technical terms used by Lewis in describing social structure and organisation in Arabia. "Arab society," he writes, "on the eve of Islam consisted of kings, feudalism, vassals, peasants, and tribes" (*ibid*:25). "Feudalism", "vassals", and "peasants" are the vocabulary of medieval Europe. I seriously doubt if the concept of feudalism is applicable within the highly developed tribal structure in Arabia (before or after Islam). In any case the two would find it difficult to co-exist ("Kings" and "feudalism" and segmentary tribal groups are at different ends of the social spectrum). Feudalism, as we know, is a discrete social category with associated characteristics. It is the wrong time, place, and people for such concepts. Lewis, a few pages later contradicts himself when he — correctly this time — talks of the domination of "Bedouin tribalism" (*ibid*:29).

Even today Orientalists in a hangover from a past age continue to offend Muslims by the use of "Mohammedanism" for Muslims (see the title of Gibb 1980, and of Grunebaum 1951). Such perception affects those who look to the Orientalists for guidance. The Oxford dictionary still uses the word "Mohammedanism" in spite of its obvious odium for Muslims.

Of the numerous derogatory references to Muslims in Orientalist literature, let me pick a few at random to illustrate the point.[1] In the last chapter, "Assessment", of the standard biography of the Prophet in the West, the author discusses Adolf Hitler's "creative imagination" and "neurotic" character (Watt 1978:239). He relates these to the "neurosis" of his followers. This is immediately followed by a discussion of the creative imagination of the Prophet: the point being made to a Western audience — the book was first published just 16 years after the Second World War and hysteria about the Germans still remained — is as explicit as it is crude.[2] Another social scientist (Patai 1969) sets out to demonstrate why and how Muslim society responds to the fuehrer-type leader (the Hitler motif is, once again, introduced).

1. For a recent — and exceedingly sharp — attack on Islam see Laffin, 1981.
2. For a direct comparison of Hitler and Ayatullah Khomeini see Carpozi 1979.

The Orientalists have neither tired nor relented. In a new work, *Hagarism: The Making of the Islamic World,* the authors, Crone and Cook, attack the very core of Islam[1] (1980). It is the traditional Orientalist attack on the authenticity of prophethood with a more sophisticated and academic approach.

Claiming to have discovered original contemporary documents Crone and Cook put forward a thesis that the Prophethood of Islam belonged to Caliph 'Umar al Faruq (RAA,[2] d.24AH/644AC). They argue that the Prophet Muhammad (SAAS)[3] was sent to preach the coming of Hazrat Umar but decided to appropriate the role for himself. The authors further challenge the historicity of the *hijrah* and its date 622 (Crone and Cook 1980:9). Academic neutrality is abandoned in their dislike for Islam. In a discussion of comparative intellectual trends in Islam, Judaism, and Christianity the authors conclude: "The only obverse to the *gravitas* of Muslims is the giggling of their womenfolk" (*ibid*:147). The authors are themselves on record as suggesting the book will cause offense to Muslims: "This is a book written by infidels for infidels" (*ibid*:8). They do not wish for academic dialogue.

For Muslims it is easy to dismiss the book as nonsense.[4] I disagree. With its academic pretensions (written by Professors of London University and published by Cambridge University Press) Islamic scholars would do well to prepare a reply. If not, their silence will be taken as an incapacity to prepare a suitable answer.

The Orientalists compare the Prophet's age as one of "violence" and "barbarism" to theirs of "gentleness" and "peace"! Montgomery Watt — suggesting the death of Kab ibn al Ashraf, an enemy of Islam, was instigated by the Prophet — observes, "In the gentler... age in which we live men look askance at such conduct, particularly in a religious leader" (Watt 1978:128-9). He compares his own age with that of the Prophet's and concludes that "in Muhammad's age and country such behavior was quite normal" (*ibid.*).

What, Watt is saying, can we expect from people who had no "common decency" (*ibid*:173)? "We" as Edward Said has alerted the West, "are rational and virtuous and they — the people of the Orient — are irrational and depraved."

Taking this cue from Orientalists, certain anthropologists have employed the "Peace and War" distinction to classify "primitive" tribes and "civilized" nations (Sahlins 1968).[5] Tribesmen are constantly killing each

---

1. Also see Crone 1980.

2. *Radiya Allahu 'Anhu* (May God be pleased with him).

3. *Salla Allahu 'Alayhi wa Sallam* (May God bless and favor him).

4. In fact this was precisely the answer I was given by the Central Education Secretary of the Government of Pakistan when I discussed the book with him. Modern Muslim intellectuals, too, appear to have lost patience with the West (Ahmed 1976, Gauhar 1978).

5. "In its broadest terms the contrast between tribe and civilization is between War and Peace... lacking these institutional means and guarantees, tribesmen live in a condition of War, and War limits the scale, complexity, and all round richness of their culture, and accounts for some of their more 'curious' customs". (Sahlins 1968:5).

other or engaging in "War". Civilized nations, on the other hand, live in "Peace". The comparison never fails to amuse me. It is made by members of the civilized nations who in this century alone have plunged the entire world into wars that lasted for years at a toll of millions of lives.

We are still paying for those years of global madness. The scale, organization — and savagery — of the two World Wars has never been matched before in human history. And today we may be drifting to a Third War — a nuclear one this time — again fought by the advanced and civilized nations of the world.

Is the Orientalist really serious about the gentleness of our age? How do we explain the millions "gently" killed by Stalin, Hitler, Mao and Pol Pot. Hitler is accused of having exterminated between five and six million Jews alone in the most savage and unprecedented manner, an event which has permanently scarred the consciousness of modern man. This from a "gentle" age characterised by "common decency". In contrast let me cite the example of "primitive" people at war.

When the Prophet (SAAS) finally reconquered Makkah — after suffering extreme personal humiliation from the city — he forgave all those who wished to live in peace. A general amnesty was declared and apart from a few criminals, no one was killed. The conquest of Makkah — a turning point in the history of Islam — involved the death of less than 30 people in combat (and during the march on the city the Prophet's humanity was undiminished and displayed itself when he ordered the protection of a bitch who had given birth to new puppies). During the Prophet's entire career and campaigns, only about a thousand men — Muslims and non-Muslims — died. A cheap price for one of the world's greatest revolutions. Be that as it may, the myth of anarchy and instability among Muslim groups persisted and persists.

Perhaps it was the Victorian emphasis on order and stability that was reflected in the perception of Muslim tribal groups. These tribal groups were seen as intrinsically turbulent and unstable "ordered anarchies". Violence was seen as characteristic of society. I agree with Professor Abdullah Laroui, the Moroccan historian, that the colonial cliché describing hill tribes — "a scattering of tribes killing each other" — was the aim not the cause of colonialism (1977). Nonetheless the "anarchic" perception of tribal society is a legacy which persists in contemporary anthropology: "North Arabian Bedouin culture turned in large part upon the notion that violence lay at the center of political life. Men tended to think of themselves, their possessions, and their relationships in terms of this violence" (Meeker 1979:19). And "the Cyrenaican Bedouin often perceive the entire domain of political experience as a wild world of brutality and savagery" (*ibid.*:207). Similarly, Fredrik Barth examining the Swat Pukhtuns found them ceaselessly and insatiably engaged in "attacking", "seizing", and "killing" each other (Barth 1972).

And the end is not yet in sight. The Orientalist scholars — Arberry, Gibb, Lewis, Von Gunebaum, Watt — have provided the academic base for most of anthropology. Also Richard Tapper's work leans heavily on that of the Orientalists such as Lambton (Tapper 1979).

Younger anthropologists, who write with elegance (Meeker 1979) and sympathy (Eickelman 1981)[1] of their groups, nonetheless have not been able to entirely free themselves of the Oriental heritage.[2] For Meeker, who uses Musil's material extensively, the world of the Bedouin remains anarchic (see quotations from his work above). Eickelman's comprehensive summary of Middle East anthropology relies heavily on Orientalist sources too (Eickelman 1981). Eickelman acknowledges this fact by calling his chapter — without, I am sure, being fully aware of its implication — on the Orientalists, "Intellectual Predecessors". Both cite Doughty, whose hatred of Islam bordered on the pathological, with high regard.

Women studies — or more correctly — studies by Western women of Muslim women — are no exception to the traditional Orientalist image of Muslim society. A recent study of Muslim women in Delhi is called *Frogs in a Well* (Jeffrey 1980). I am sure no women — Muslim or otherwise — would take kindly to the imagery of the metaphor. It reflects the ethnocentric arrogance of the scholar. (For other studies of Muslim women see Beck, Fernea, and Keddie.)

Even some of the work of the great Western scholars has recently been analysed as prejudiced against Islam. Bryan Turner's book *Weber and Islam* (1974) clearly pointed out Weber's personal prejudices which led him to certain conclusions regarding Islam, and in particular the person of the Prophet (SAAS).

It is little wonder that Professor Fazlur Rahman, himself once under attack from more right-wing Islamic scholars in Pakistan, doubts the impartiality of Western scholarship on Islam (Rahman 1982). Let me turn to a technical discussion in the discipline.

Fredrik Barth has been accused by me of reductionism in his portrayal of the Swat Pukhtuns (Ahmed 1976). Barth, responding to the criticism, revisited Swat. The visit did little to change his ideas (Barth 1981, Vol II).[3] He provides us with a lengthy example — "new" ethnography — purporting to explain his thesis. The driver of the bus he was on refused to give way to another van on the Nowshera bridge, an old pre-Independence one-lane railway bridge (*ibid.*:131-2, 163). Both held their ground and the situation, made tense by the arrival of a train, was diffused after considerable delay. Barth sees "deep structures" in the incident. This then, is serious anthropology explaining human behavior among Pukhtuns.

If I were to cite examples of bad drivers or more accurately — bad-mannered drivers — from England or the USA, would they support a more

1. Eickelman, in a gesture of affection for a departed colleague, dedicates his book to the Egyptian anthropologist Abdul Hamid el-Zein.
2. For a recent historical study still not entirely free of Orientalism, see Hodgson (1974).
3. It is neither possible nor appropriate to enter into a theoretical debate here. I shall do so in a separate paper (Ahmed forthcoming "The Reconsideration of Swat Pathans: A Reply to Fredrik Barth").

general thesis on Western society? I think not. The example is thus parody not science — and what does the construction of a new dual carriageway recently at Nowshera do to Barth's thesis?

For Pehrson and Barth the harsh desert fieldwork conditions (the former died in the field) among the Baluch were made worse by their perception of the Baluch as an unpleasant people. Baluch etiquette reflected "hollowness", and Baluch "intimate life" was one of "deceit" (Barth in Pehrson 1966: vii). They found the Baluch "suspicious" — a word which occurs frequently in the book (Pehrson 1966).

For Hobbes the condition of man "is a condition of war, of everyone against everyone". Barth's perception of Muslim society is Hobbesian: Muslim life is "solitary, poor, nasty, brutish and short". The Hobbesian view of life is not unnaturally reflected in the work of Mrs. Fredrik Barth — who was one of Professor Barth's students.

Mrs. Barth on the basis of interviewing females — in this case the poor women of Cairo — concludes that Muslim women are exceedingly "suspicious". She also finds they spend their time in back-biting, intriguing, and squabbling (Wikan 1977). In Cairo we are presented with a female mirror-image of the belligerent Pukhtun, who is forever "attacking", "seizing", and "killing". Man is merely the expression of the methodological individualist.

Are we being presented empirically observed social reality or simply the perception of a husband-wife team imposing their theoretical models at random on the Muslim world? On the basis of Barth's Swat material I would be justified in assuming the latter. I would be interested to hear the comments of independent native critics on the work of the Barths elsewhere in the Muslim world.[1]

Professor Barth spent most of his professional life writing and lecturing about Muslim groups. I am not objecting to his ideas about those groups. He is perfectly entitled to his views. I do object to the arrogance implied by those views. And my objection raises sadness in me rather than indignation. Sadness because my discipline — anthropology — is belittled. It is reduced to a parody and weak shadow of Orientalism. Edward Said would be roused to say that this is vintage "Orientalism".

Surely Barth does not wish to suggest that all Swat Pukhtuns do with their time is "attack" and "kill". This is one aspect of their lives. Unfortunately his data convey this impression. Even the *hujra*, the guest house, the social center of hospitality, guests, folk-song etc. is for Barth reduced simply to another political instrument and part of political strategy. It is the traditional Orientalist view of tribal Muslim groups forever absorbed in "war", their society forever "anarchic".

Frederik Bailey, following Barth, goes one step further. To him

1. By discovering a third sex; the male transsexual prostitute (the *khanith*), in Oman, Wikan sparked off an academic controversy within anthropology (in *MAN* throughout its 1978 issues) and I am told by colleagues a different, less academic, controversy in Oman.

Pukhtun society resembles the Mafia (Bailey 1970). An entire Code (the Pukhtunwali), and entire body of culture, folklore and literature of a highly developed tribal society which has perpetuated itself for at least five centuries is reduced to a modern Western urban gangster civilization. When I pointed these facts out, some of my Western critics were quick to suggest I was outraged by adverse images of the Pukhtuns. I, it was suggested, was from the area and therefore extra-sensitive about perception of its people.[1] But it was as an anthropologist, that I was appalled at the poor methodology involved in arriving at such judgments. Some of the colonial officers and Orientalists appear more balanced and fair when commenting on "primitive" and "savage" groups.

Serious doubts have been raised on the few occasions Muslim anthropologists have critically analyzed Western anthropologists on their home ground. Talal Asad (1975) made telling criticism of Abner Cohen's work among Arab villages in Israel (Cohen 1965). Unfortunately, the criticism of "native" anthropologists is sometimes easily misunderstood. When I suggested we refer to the holistic Islamic framework (Islam as culture and politics) when examining Muslim tribal groups (Ahmed 1976), I was criticized for attacking Western anthropologists and colonialism (Anderson 1981). My work was seen as an Islamic challenge.

But not all non-Muslim writing is offensively critical. The work of other younger anthropologists is enhanced by sympathy for the people they write of, for example, Fischer's recent study of Iran, its religion and religious leaders (1980)[2] and Singer's of the Pukhtuns (1982). The methodological direction indicated by the work of these anthropologists may break the impasse imposed on the discipline by Orientalism. Interestingly, the two main broad divisions in anthropology discussed above appear to be divided by the Atlantic: Fischer, the American professor at Harvard is a cultural anthropologist and Singer, the Oxford anthropologist, is a social anthropologist.

One cannot escape the conclusion arrived at by Edward Said that anthropologists to be included in the list of Orientalists are defined as "anyone who teaches, writes about, or researches the Orient" (Said 1978:2).

When the authors of Hagarism attack the Prophet (SAAS) and the very foundation of Islam or — less seriously — Western anthropologists equate entire Muslim societies to the Mafia, ought Muslims to bury their heads in the sand and pretend they do not hear these voices? Should they simply reject Western — or non-Muslim — scholarship by banning its entry into their countries? If so, do they build an intellectual iron curtain around their societies? Or ought they to assess, argue, synthesize and then prepare and reply in terms of an "Islamic Anthropology". One aim of this paper is to illuminate the above questions.

1. R. Tapper review of Ahmed (1980) in *Asian Affairs,* London, October 1981.
2. Fischer dedicated his book "to the warm courageous and complex people of Iran" — at a time when the crisis of the hostages in America was at its height and so was, consequently, anti-Iranian feeling.

PART TWO

V. ISLAMIC ANTHROPOLOGY

A. The Problem of Definition

It would appear from the previous section that anthropology is, if not a child, a creation of the West and more specifically Western imperialism. This is not so. The work of Ibn Khaldun is reflected — with theoretical frame and supporting data — in that of some of the most influential contemporary Western theorists including Karl Marx, Max Weber, Vilfredo Pareto and Ernest Gellner. Weber's typology of leadership, Pareto's circulation of elites, and Gellner's pendulum swing theory of Muslim society betray the influence of Ibn Khaldun. It is indeed a tragedy that the science of sociology or anthropology did not develop after Ibn Khaldun. And Ibn Khaldun was not alone. There were al Biruni, Ibn Battutar and al Mas'udi, to name a few.

Of these perhaps al Biruni (973-1048) deserves the title of father of anthropology (I have explored this in "Al Biruni: the First Anthropologist" 1984). If anthropology is a science based on extended participant observation of (other) cultures using the data collected, for value-neutral, dispassionate analysis employing the comparative method, then al Biruni is indeed an anthropologist of the highest contemporary standards (al Biruni 1984; Said 1979; Said & Zahid 1981). His work on (Hindu) India — *Kitab al Hind* — remains one of the most important source books for South Asia. The most perceptive of contemporary Hindu scholars, including mavericks like Nirad Chaudhari, quote him approvingly (1965). So, almost a thousand years before Malinowski and Geertz, al Biruni was establishing the science of anthropology. Therefore, the study of society by Muslims, Islamic sociology or anthropology, is not a new or Western science.

We may define Islamic anthropology loosely as the study of Muslim groups by scholars committed to the universalistic principles of Islam — humanity, knowledge, tolerance — relating micro village tribal studies in particular to the larger historical and ideological frames of Islam. Islam is here understood not as theology but sociology. The definition thus does not preclude non-Muslims.

Certain conceptual points must first be clarified. What is the world view of the Muslim anthropologist? In the ideal the Muslim orders his life according to the will of God. In actuality this may not be so. Does he see

56

society as motivated by the desire to perform the will of God or not? If so, the Muslim must strive to bring the actual into accord with the ideal.

Let us pose these questions in the context of the two major — sometimes overlapping — theoretical positions in the Western social sciences. These divisions are between the "methodological individualists" and the "methodological holists". Briefly, the individualists examine man in society as an actor maximizing and optimizing. Social interaction is seen as a series of transactions in which "value gained and lost" is recorded in individual "ledgers" (Barth 1966:4).

The "holists", on the other hand, view man as motivated by configurations of economy and society which transcend the individual. These divisions are not rigid and are made more complex by the different schools of anthropology.

Such debates must be directed to scientific inquiry in order to discover the dynamics of society. For society is dynamic and studies of social phenomena which are not directed towards clarifying it are reduced to academic exercises.

Which framework is applicable when analyzing a Muslim social actor? Does he behave as an individualist recording units of value gained and lost in a personal ledger? Or does he respond to social configurations of which he is part? With Muslims we may suggest the latter.

Islam teaches us to deal with the major concern of human beings which is to relate to our environment. And our relationships with people — individuals and groups — are the main features of our environment. Islam, then is a social religion. The implications for the Muslim are clear. He is part of the *ummah*, the community, to which he gives loyalty and which provides him with social identity. In the ideal, he belongs in part to his immediate group, in part to the larger *ummah*.

For the Muslim, rules of marriage, inheritance and an entire code — covering the most intimate details of human behavior — are laid down explicitly. The organization of society and the behavior of its members are predetermined. For Muslims, therefore, the dilemmas of this world are reduced. Man's mission is to reconcile society with the instructions of God. Debates between one or another school of thought thus become merely academic exercises.

Life, God has repeated, has not been created in jest. It is a struggle to better humanity, to improve the moral quality of our brief span on earth. The struggle to do so — the *jihad* — must be maintained.

The Muslim remains part of the *ummah*, the community. A too blatant expression of individual ambitious desire will provoke disapproval from the community. Which is not to say individuals do not break rules or behave in an entirely non-Muslim manner. But we are concerned with Muslim groups and not individuals. This social ethos is in contrast to the West where man is an individual first and last. Politics, business and even private life in the West are an expression of this individuality. It is this contrast which sometimes makes it difficult for the two civilizations to see eye to eye on certain key issues.

How do Muslims tackle the subject of anthropology of Islam as Muslims — as believers. Ali Shariati has attempted an answer: "Religion is, therefore, a road or a path, leading from clay to God and conveying man from vileness, stagnation and ignorance, from the lowly life of clay and satanic character, towards exaltation, motion, vision, the life of the spirit and divine character. If it succeeds in doing so, then it is religion in truth. But if it does not, then either you have chosen the wrong path, or you are making wrong use of the right path." (Shariati 1979: 94).

Anthropology, I am arguing, can assist in illuminating "the right path". But the primary problem before us is not the balancing of options but finding out what they are.

The two myths pertaining to the Muslim social world which continue to provide material to attack Muslims are the status of women (their lack of rights, their suppression and, connected to this, polygamy in the society) and the continuing tyranny, anarchy, and despotism of Muslim politics (the paperback version of Wittfogel's *Oriental Despotism* displays a picture of a mosque on its cover, 1981). We have seen how anthropologists often reflect the second in their depiction of Muslim political life. The first point is less well advertised, as the literature has been largely by male anthropologists who have had little access to Muslim women.

Minor religious injunctions or customs are exaggerated and ridicule Islam. For instance, Muslims are prohibited from eating pork as it is not considered *halal* or pure. Many other animals are also considered impure or *haram*. This is one of the features best known about Muslim by non-Muslims. A minor social injunction has become a major theological issue (pig taboo among Muslims was the theme of an academic controversy in *Current Anthropology* recently). The prohibition is a subject of caricature and satire. It has become one of the symbols dividing the Western (pork-eating) and Muslim (non pork-eating) world.

What methodological position would Islamic anthropology adopt to tackle these issues? One answer — and perhaps the easiest way out — is to be eclectic. But eclecticism is self-defeating, not because there is only one direction in which it is heuristically useful to move, but so many. We must choose — what Shariati calls — "the right path".

There has been a suggestion by Muslim anthropologists that there is not one Islam but many Islams (el-Zein 1974, 1977), a suggestion taken up by Western anthropologists (Eickelman 1981). I disagree with this position. There is only one Islam, and there can be only one Islam, but there are many Muslim societies. We must then not look for numerous "Islams" but we must attempt to place the multitude of Muslim societies within the framework of one universal Islam.

In a paper written a few years ago, I had argued that the romantic view of the tribesman created as a result of the colonial encounter was false (Ahmed 1978). The view did not take into account the real hardships the tribesmen faced in militarily challenging the Imperial power. To the

Pukhtuns in the Tribal Areas, for instance, there was no romance in fighting the British. Barbed wires and bombed civilian populations do not win friends. For the Pukhtuns the encounter remained an unceasing struggle for religion and freedom.

The debate between those examining tribal or nomad groups "romantically" versus those who see them realistically persists in modern anthropology. The Bedouins of Saudi Arabia provide a contemporary example. Lancaster, an Englishman, sees the Bedouins as "the noble savage", embodying the virtues of the desert (1980, 1981) in contrast to the American anthropologist Cole (1975) — one of the few Western anthropologists allowed to do fieldwork in Saudi Arabia. Muslim intellectuals do not necessarily harbor romantic views of tribesmen. To them Islam — and Islamic culture — lie in the city (Ajami 1981: 103-4). The "romantic" image obfuscates the real problems of the tribesmen. The tribesman cannot ignore or reject the twentieth century; he cannot will away the state he is part of.

To understand better, segmentary tribal social structure and organization with reference to the Pukhtun, I had suggested a taxonomic exercise (Ahmed 1976, 1980a). Pukhtun society may be divided into two discrete categories. Each category is symbolized by a key concept, *nang* (honour) in one and *qalang* (rents and taxes) in the other case. *Nang* and *qalang* are the major conative and affective symbols in society. *Nang* society, based largely in the Tribal Areas, is acephalous, egalitarian, and placed in low production zones. *Qalang* society is ranked, literate and dependent on large irrigated estates. *Qalang* creates superior and subordinate social roles. *Nang* and *qalang* are categories which are useful when looking at Muslim groups elsewhere (Ahmed and Hart 1983).

In a recent study I have suggested we examine not the macro level of society — dynasties, armies, finances — nor the typical anthropological village but an intermediate level — the district (Ahmed 1982 b, 1983). On this level three key and distinct categories of society interact: the representatives of central government (whether army or civil), traditional leaders (based on land or genealogy) and religious leaders (usually the *mullahs*). For this purpose we may construct the Islamic district paradigm (Islam here is understood in a sociological not theological sense). In particular, roles such as that of the *mullah,* one of the least understood and least studied must be carefully researched. We have two distinct images of the *mullah*. One derives from the Western prototype, the "Mad Mullah", from Swat to Sudan. The image of the fanatic was fostered by the British as the *mullahs* stood against them when other groups in society had quietly acquiesced. The other image is that of saintly figures incapable of wrong, as suggested by Muslim writers. The truth is somewhere in between.[1] It is at this district level of society where we may predict and foretell the shape of

1. For a contemporary political study of a *mullah* operating within traditional tribal networks in Waziristan, see my *Religion and Politics in Muslim Society: Order and Conflict in Pakistan,* Cambridge University Press, 1983.

things to come in Muslim society. The Islamic district paradigm will help us do so.

A perception such as that of the Orientalist anthropologist re-opens a fundamental question regarding anthropology. Is one function of anthropology to serve as a bridge between different cultural systems helping us to understand others and thereby ourselves? If so, such perceptions as that of Barth, may not be the best material for the bridge. Some third-world anthropologists would argue that it is already too late for any bridge-building exercises (see Asad 1973). However scientific the analysis, human beings are sensitive to cultural arrogance disguised as scientific jargon.

The anthropologist in some ways is an ambassador of his world to the village he is visiting. He not only interprets the native group to his world but his own world to them. If he is not conscious of his relationship he may create problems for future social scientists in that area or working with his group.

The question raises a related issue. Is good anthropology — from the point of view of the native, at least — sympathetic anthropology? Not necessarily. Anthropologists must record society as it *is* not as it *should be*. But I think it is imperative that anthropology be fair. Not only the warts on the face of society need to be emphasized. It is for this reason we may today read *The Sanusi of Cyrenaica* (Evans-Pritchard 1973) and find it a fair account although it was written by a colonial officer a generation ago. Some understanding of the virtues of a people especially as anthropologists see them, along with a scientific analysis, are important to the discipline.[1]

It is worth noting that anthropology as a discipline is yet to grow in the Muslim world. Muslim anthropologists of stature are few and far between. The two outstanding examples are Nur Yalman of Turkey and Imtiaz Ahmed of India. Nur is almost unique in that his topic of study was a

---

1. Not only are some members of the First World — anthropologists and others — guilty of lack of sympathy for the Third World. The colonial mentality was never a monopoly of the West. The *kala sahib* — black sahib — one feature of Empire in South Asia, still lives. A good example of a Third World writer living in and writing for the First World is V.S. Naipaul. His characteristic features — sharp powers of observation and brilliant skill at description combined with cynicism and contempt for his subject — are displayed to the full in his new book on Muslim society (1981). His method is what I would call "First World contemporary colonial", that is, fly into the local Intercontinental hotel, pick up a taxi and drive around for a few hours or days picking up trivia before moving to the next place.

In the course of his interviews, he uses the most objectionable methods such as lying — as to Ayatullah Shirazi in Iran (Naipaul 1981: 49-53) — and repeating private conversations confided by his hosts whether Indian housewives or petty officials in Pakistan. To him these people, whose lives are sunk in personal and public chaos and irreversible poverty, appear to do little more than, hawk, fart, nose-pick, deceive (themselves), and despair. Despair — the word sounding like a death-knell — is repeated in his work. His people are caricatures of a caricature.

This is Naipaul's world view of the Third World. Muslims are no exception. Yet nowhere have I read an expression of personal gratitude for people who are with such limited resources so generously hospitable to him; no word of sympathy for their aspirations and struggle; no suggestion of hope for their goals. The "First World contemporary colonial" visits these people with a set objective in mind: he is extracting a new book from their lives. He cannot be distracted by humanity and its suffering (For a rebuttal of Naipaul by a Muslim scholar see Khurshid Ahmad 1982).

Buddhist village in Sri Lanka. He is unique in that for once in the contemporary world Islam was observing and not being observed. Imtiaz Ahmed, an Indian Muslim examines his own people. He reflects the major sociological problems confronting Indian Muslims, in particular the continuing interaction with the larger Hindu cultural system. His work discusses the growth of caste among Muslims.[1]

The Muslim intellectual confronting the world today is sometimes moved to despair. He is ill-equipped to face it. His vulnerability diminishes him in his own eyes. He wanders between two worlds, one dead, the other powerless to be born. His wounds are largely self-inflicted. At the root of his intellectual malaise lies his incapacity to come to terms with Islam in the twentieth century.

The aim of anthropology remains to move from the specific to the general, to draw universal conclusions from specific situations. If so, is "Islamic anthropology" only for Islam or Muslims? No. The lessons we may learn will be methodologically valid for other world religious systems specifically and Third World cultural systems generally.

B. Muslim Societies

Let me briefly attempt a taxonomy of Muslim society — providing models with associated characteristics — based on historical sequences and social structure and organization. The taxonomy of Muslim society will illustrate the variety of structures and therefore the complexity of the problem. The models generally provide a chronological sequence corresponding with broad periods in Muslim history. But the categories are neither complete nor incontrovertible. The taxonomy is merely a starting point for a sociological discussion of Islamic anthropology.

The first, primordial model, one which is associated with early Islam and continues until today, is "tribal segmentary Islam". This category may include the Bedouin, the Berber, and the Pukhtun. These tribes are spread from one end of North Africa to North West Pakistan but the model is recognizable and in many ways similar. A sense of tribal identity and an understanding of the tribal code are highly developed and the world is seen in relationship to one's place on the genealogical charter. It was perhaps on account of his awareness of this form of social organization that the Prophet (SAAS) in his well known *hadith* warned that there were no genealogies in Islam. Islam then, transcends tribal loyalties.

The second category provides a model which may be called the "Ottoman" or the "cantonment" model of Islam and this contrasts sharply

---

1. The name of Muhammad Mauroof (Professor and Chairman, Department of Anthropology, Cheyney State University, Cheyney, PA) author of "Elements For an Islamic Anthropology" in I.R. al Faruqi and A.O. Naseef, eds., *Social and Natural Sciences: The Islamic Perspective* (London: Hodder and Stoughton, 1981, pp.116-139) should be mentioned — Ed.

with the previous model. Chronologically, this model evolved during the zenith of Islamic history. The Ottomans had hit upon a solution which rather neatly solved the tribal problem. They selected administrators from one part of their empire and gave them charges in distant parts. Loyalties with tribal kin or land were therefore eliminated. The administrator served only the empire. To some extent the other great empires of Islam, such as the Safawis and the Mughals, also adopted the 'Uthmanli (Ottoman) model.

More lasting than the 'Uthmanli model were "the Great-River Islamic civilizations". These civilizations, along the Indus, the Tigris and the Nile produced societies and dynasties with characteristic splendor, palaces, standing armies, and vast bureaucracies. Their rise and decline sometimes coincided with Islamic empires mentioned above, sometimes not. One aspect of these civilizations has been termed "Oriental Despotism" (Wittfogel 1957). With the slow process of decay, Islamic societies fell prey to expanding Western powers eager for colonies and markets.

The fourth category (covering the last two centuries) may be termed "Islam under Western imperialism". The West conquered and colonized the Muslims. In this phase a determined attempt was made by the West to portray Islam as stagnant and decadent. Along with discrediting or smashing the centers of Islam, other more interesting attempts were made to create alternative societies.

The most famous examples of these were the canal colonies of the Punjab in the late last century. A model province was ordered for South Asia. Virgin land was provided to settlers but the village scheme reflected the South Asian caste and structure. The *choudhry* — or *lambardar* — headed the village. Beneath him were members of the dominant *bardari* or *qom* (tribe or lineage). At the bottom of the ladder were the *kammis* — the occupational groups — the barbers and carpenters. The *mullah,* the religious functionary, who symbolizes Islamic function in village society, was deliberately included among the *kammis* as a sign of humiliation. It was made explicit that Muslim rule was over. The *mullah,* the man who led the Muslim prayers in the mosque, was clearly subordinated to the *choudhry* or the *lambardar* of the village who was appointed by the British. Perhaps the harshness was due to British incapacity to deal with other altogether different category of *mullahs,* those among tribal groups who led revolts throughout the empire. The British dismissed the leaders of Islamic revolts against them as mere fanatics. The "Mad Mullah" was a handy imperial label to explain away Muslim leaders from Sudan to Swat. Until today the Mullah has not entirely shaken off his association with the *kammis* of the village (for instance in the revenue records such as the *jamabandi*).

In this phase of history the *mullah* had become a metaphor for Islam, his place in the village hierarchy a reflection of his destiny and that of his religion.

"Re-emergent Islam" is the fifth and contemporary model of Islam. Re-emergent Islam in the contemporary Muslim world is perhaps best symbolized by Pakistan both in its moments of glory and its moments of pain. The very creation of Pakistan itself was a living symbol of a renascent Islam and its power to mobilize followers. The name of its capital further symbolizes its self-conscious destiny, Islamabad — the abode of Islam. The defeat, humiliation, and physical breaking of Pakistan in 1971 was symptomatic of the counter pressures that were generated by means of this form of force and vitality by the enemies of Islamic endeavor.

It is in this phase that the immediate past is sometimes renegotiated and sometimes rejected. For instance, Lyallpur, one of the major towns of the Punjab, named after the British Governor Lyall — who was referred to earlier — has been renamed Faisalabad after the popular king Faisal of Arabia.

But perhaps Iran has surpassed Pakistan as a living symbol of Islam. However, it is too early to comment on the situation in Iran. The 1970s were — and it is predicted the 1980s will be — decades of "re-emergent Islam". This model is as dynamic and as exciting with possibilities as it is unpredictable.

But Muslim social history is not all defeat and conquest, and societies not all dynasties and tribes. Muslim society is also characterized by towns and trade (which accounts for the spread of Islam in the distant parts of Southeast Asia) and the presence of vigorous minority groups living in Thailand, China, Russia, and India.

It is no coincidence that in the Western world Islam remains weak. There are only small Islamic groups in Western Europe, North and South America, Australia and South Africa. Islam remains confined in the main to Asia and Africa.

Over the last centuries the world of Islam has rarely been tranquil. Internally it has constantly challenged and renewed itself. Religious leaders have emerged in the heart of Arabia, such as Muhammad ibn 'Abd al Wahab and Sidi al Hasan Lyusi in Morocco. Apart from these leaders who strove to reform the Muslims from within were those whose first task was to challenge the enemies of Islam. Through the ages Muslim leaders have emerged to challenge and engage those forces hostile to Islam. In the last century in South Asia, Sayyid Ahmad Barelwi, in what is now Pakistan and Hajj Shari'a Allah in Bengal, emerged to conduct *jihad*. Later in the century the Mahdi emerged in Sudan, the Sanusi in Cyrenaica, and the Akhund in Swat to organize Muslims according to Islam and fight to maintain their religious and cultural boundaries against imperial forces.

Today Muslim society is again moving. Tribes and peasant groups in the Muslim world today are changing and will continue to change rapidly.

Weber has underlined the role of the Protestant ethic in the success story of modern capitalism. Work, for its own sake, thrift, and austerity have combined to lay the foundations of capitalist society. But in parts of the Muslim world, the discovery of oil has brought new and untold riches abruptly. Wealth has been generated by forces that are not internal to the structure of society. Society is being changed as a result of economic changes which remain external. Unless anthropologists, first, analyze the social

63

situation and, second, the leaders of society utilize this knowledge, the tensions can be severe. Here, too, anthropological studies can assist in our understanding of the processes of change.

C. Society During the Time of the Prophet (SAAS)

When Muslim leaders talk about creating a perfect contemporary Muslim society, what do they mean? To assist us in building this society we may refer to the original ideal Muslim society at the time of the Prophet. But have we a clear understanding or even picture of that model? Do we know the various inter-connected parts of the structure of that society? We must clearly — and through sociological models — know about the household, the *rites de passage,* the genealogical charters related to questions of exogamy and endogamy, the role of elders, and the general code of behavior permeating society.

There are some speculatory anthropological papers on the subject (Aswad 1979, Eickelman 1967, Lagace 1957, Wold 1951). But we need a thorough study. It is fundamental to those talking of creating a contemporary Muslim society on the basis of an early Islamic model to first create a model of the original. To the best of my knowledge no such task has been attempted.[1] Related to the question of writing on early Islam is the life of the Prophet himself (SAAS).

The life of the Prophet (SAAS) needs to be produced in simple and clear terms for the contemporary generation of Muslims. As his life and example remain the primary paradigm of Islamic behavior, the exercise is vital to an understanding of Islam — both for Muslims and non-Muslims. His social roles — father, husband, friend and so on — illuminate some key principles of Islamic social behavior. How these roles relate to fathers, husbands, and friends in our world needs to be discussed and elaborated.

The traditional Islamic scholar needs to shift the personality of the Prophet (SAAS) to where it belongs — the forefront of the Islamic argument. We need to know more of him as a social person; his humility (his doubts to Hazrat Khadijah — RAA — when he received the first revelations); his humor (rebuking his closest companion Abu Bakr — RAA — who had lost his temper and was beating a man for letting a camel stray during a pilgrimage, with a smile, "Look at this pilgrim"); his humanity (forgiving Hind, who in her hatred of him ate the liver of his uncle Hamzah, the lion of Allah); his gentleness (he could not contain his tears when he told the children and wife of Ja'far ibn Abu Talib of his death); his love of children (the Madinah boy with whom he joked — and comforted, when the boy's pet nightingale died); and his kindness to animals (posting a man to guard the puppies of a bitch who had given birth on the way to the conquest

1. This is an exercise I hope to conduct in the near future *The Social Structure and Organization of Early Muslim Society* (Ahmed forthcoming).

of Makkah). These examples speak of a man of extraordinary perception, goodness and gentleness.

A biography written by Muslims for Muslims is needed. And in spite of the need for such a biography those worthy of the subject are few and far between; of these al Faruqi's translation of Haykal (1976) and Lings, (1983) may be mentioned. A notable — if somewhat apologetic — attempt was made a century ago by Sayyid Amir Ali. Muhammad Zafarullah Khan's biography of the Prophet — 1980 — presents problems for those Muslims who hold the author's sect as outside the pale of Islam.

Some Muslim biographers have rarely risen over simple hagiography. For our purposes what is needed is sociology not hagiography. On the other hand, the standard Western biographies — and some of the material is based on extensive research — are for the most part a generation old or older, and reflect some of the traditional animosity to their subject (Andrae 1936, Archer 1924, Bell 1926, Gibb 1980, Muir 1858-61, Rodinson 1980 and Watt 1953, 1956, 1978). Watt's biographies still remain the standard Western work on the subject. There are a few "modern" biographies, such as Rodinson (1980) which relies on psychological analysis.[1] Recent Western scholarship appears undecided on how to treat the life of the Prophet.

VI. CONCLUSION
A. Recommendations

Muslims cannot dismiss Western — or more correctly non-Muslim — scholarship out of hand. They must come to terms with it. For instance, anyone reading about the Pukhtun will probably come to them through Caroe. The inaccuracies will thus be perpetuated. The inaccuracies extend even to the name "Pathan" for "Pukhtun" or "Pushtun", a name invented and now confirmed for that tribal group. If Muslims are to object to such scholarship, they can only do so by creating their own alternative scholarship rather than by verbally berating Western scholarship.

Anthropology is important to the study of Muslim society. It has much to offer in helping to understand and solve contemporary social problems. For instance, I have argued that the distribution of aid to the Afghan refugees in Pakistan would benefit if anthropological expertise were available (Ahmed 1981a). Sometimes the lacuna between the "actual" and the "ideal" in Muslim society is wide. A good example is the actual status of Muslim women among certain groups, which contrasts with the ideal (Ahmed A. and Z. 1981). Anthropological studies can help to compare the two positions in the hope of attempting a bridge. Take another example, ethnic tensions which are often read as expressions of political secession in most nation states, may be minimized by a national understanding of different local cultures and their social characteristics.

1. Rodinson uses anthropological arguments in his discussion of "the Arabs" (1981).

Muslims are not living in a social vacuum. They are living in a world sometimes operating on different levels within their own society, and outside their society, on levels that are sometimes hostile, sometimes neutral. They have to meet the challenge on every one of these levels. For better or for worse, Muslims are being "observed".[1] And the observations indicate lack of understanding and are usually hostile (Said 1981).

Keeping the above in mind, it is therefore recommended that:

1) A simple, lucid sociological account of the life of the Prophet (SAAS) be prepared by a Muslim. The book should address a wide audience — both Muslim and non-Muslim — and neither be too academic nor too abstruse (see above discussion)[2]

2) One major standard anthropological text book of high standard should be produced and then translated into the major languages of the Muslim world. It should be used at the BA level and include sections on each major cultural zone.

3) Anthropological monographs on each major Islamic region are produced for distribution in the Muslim world.[3] Initially, Morocco for the Maghrib, Pakistan for South Asia, and Indonesia for Southeast Asia as distinct cultural-geographical types may be selected. These monographs should be simple, lucid, with attractive photographs and used in colleges and universities.

4) Visits of Muslim anthropologists within Muslim countries should be arranged and encouraged and joint projects initiated. For instance, the study of the Berbers and the Pukhtuns is a logical and exciting study.

5) Long-term studies should be conducted comparing the major social categories which would help us better understand and reach conclusions regarding Muslim society and its immediate contemporary problems.

The social categories to be examined could be peasants, tribes and cities. For the first, I recommend a village in Pakistan (preferably the most populous Province, Punjab) and an Egyptian village typically dependent on irrigated networks. For the tribes, the Berbers and the Pukhtuns would be a natural study, and for the cities, Cairo, Madinah and Lahore.

6) Practical and development-orientated social studies should be framed in order to enable us to better plan for Muslim society in the twentieth century.

1. Clifford Geertz, one of the more sympathetic observers, titled his book, *"Islam Observed"* (Geertz 1968). The interest in Islam has affected publishing. Studies of Muslim society are now big publishing business. Publishers assess that to add "Islam" to a title is to guarantee sales. Hence titles like *"Islam and Development"* (Esposito 1980) have appeared recently in the market. But not only the West is guilty of commercializing Islam: Pakistan film-makers recently produced a film with the unlikely title of *"Khuda aur Mahabbat"* — God and love — (starring Pakistan's most popular actor, Muhammad Ali, and actresss Babra Sharif).
2. For example, as a model, see Professor I. al Faruqi's translation of Haykal's *"The Life of Muhammad"* (1976). For interesting work along these lines, see some of the recent publications of the newly formed Islamic associations like The Islamic Foundation, Leicester; the Institute of Policy Studies, Islamabad and the International Institute of Islamic Thought, Washington.
3. For an attempt at bringing together the Islamic tribes under one cover in anthropology, see Ahmed and Hart 1983.

7) I recommend that the ethnographic and anthropological content from the writings of the great Muslim writers is extracted and compiled in a discrete set of volumes.[1] In this exercise classic Islamic scholars will have to assist the anthropologist.

A great store of anthropology exists in the writing of the classic Muslim scholars. It is disguised as history in one text, as memoirs in another, and straightforward ethnography in the third.

Such academic endeavor will assist us in creating a core of Islamic anthropological literature for the future. I agree with Arab intellectuals that we must possess major journals and create "educational institutions capable of challenging places like Oxford, Harvard or UCLA" (Said 1978:323). Otherwise Muslims will continue to be subordinated to the intellectual trends of the west.

B. Conclusion

By failing to predict the contemporary Islamic re-emergence or assess its importance, Western scholars of Islam and its peoples were encouraged to make one of their most spectacular mistakes in recent times. They assumed secular trends in Muslim society as a logical development after the Second World War. Such was the direction pointed out by the Orientalists a generation ago (Gibb 1980). However, the scholars of modern times seem to follow blindly in the footpaths of their predecessors and fall into the same errors. A Western scholar of Iran, for example, wrote recently that "Although it is difficult to be certain, the trend seems to be away from physical resistance movements such as those during Muharram of 1963, and more towards ideological resistance through involvement and participation in the decision-making apparatus of the government". His paper concluded thus, "Religiously oriented individuals, who may oppose the government nevertheless, join its ranks in the hope that they will have the opportunity to implement policies that will be more in accord with their view that Islam is an all-encompassing system of beliefs" (Thaiss 1978: 366). And this from an Iran expert on the eve of the religious revolution that brought down the Shah.

Muslim scholars trained in the west commit the same mistake. 'Aziz Ahmad concluded a paper on Islam in Pakistan thus: "The *ulema* having suffered a setback in 1970, Islamic socialism, in which Islam is largely decorative and diplomatic, has for the time being at least gained a complete victory over the religious parties" (Aziz Ahmad 1978: 272). The vigor of the Islamic revival has repudiated the predictions of, and surprised Islamic scholars. To his credit Clifford Geertz was one of the few Western writers

---

1. One such attempt has been made in this direction in *Muslim Society: Readings in Thought, Development and Structure,* Routledge and Kegan Paul, London (Ahmed 1982a).

who saw differently.[1]

Having conceded the vigor of the Islamic revival, Muslims must now plan directions for it in order to best utilize its finer and dynamic impulses. They must, as Shariati suggests, prepare to discover what "the right path" means today and should mean in the future.

The anthropologist would do well to remember Socrates' statement, "I am not an Athenian or a Greek, but a citizen of the World." In the end the anthropologist must transcend himself, his culture, his universe, to a position where he is able to speak to and understand those around him in terms of his special humanity irrespective of color, caste or creed.

This sentiment is a poor echo of the Prophet (SAAS) — who in his last great address spoke to mankind, "Allah has made you brethren one to another, so be not divided... An Arab has no preference over a non-Arab, nor a non-Arab over an Arab; nor is a white one to be preferred to a dark one, nor a dark one to a white one, except in righteousness."

---

1. Sarcastically, Clifford Geertz writes for the benefit of his overhasty Western colleagues: "We have a while to wait yet, I think, even in Tunisia or Egypt, before we see an explicit movement for a 'religionless Islam' advancing under the banner, 'Allah is dead' " (Geertz 1968: 115).

BIBLIOGRAPHY

Ahmad, A. 1978. Activism of the Ulema in Pakistan, in N.R. Kedaie, ed. *Scholars, Saints, and Sufis,* Berkeley: University of California Press.

Ahmad, K. 1976. *Islam: Its Meaning and Message,* London: Islamic Council of Europe.

— — — 1982. What an Islamic Journey. Review of V.S. Naipaul, 1981. *The Muslim World Book Review,* Vol. 2, No. 3, Spring.

Ahmad, S. 1977. *Class and Power in a Punjabi Village,* Monthly Review Press.

Ahmed, A.S. 1976. *Millennium and Charisma among Pathans: A Critical Essay in Social Anthropology,* London: Routledge and Kegan Paul.

— — — 1978. The Colonial Encounter on the Northwest Frontier Province: Myth and Mystification. *Journal of the Anthropological Society of Oxford,* Oxford, vol. IX, no.3.

— — — 1980. *Pukhtun Economy and Society: Traditional Structure and Economic Development in a Tribal Society,* London: Routledge and Kegan Paul.

— — — 1980b. Introduction to E. Howell. *Mizh: A Monograph on Government's Relations with the Mahsud Tribe,* Oxford in Asia Series, Karachi: Oxford University Press.

— — — 1981a. Afghan Refugees, Aid and Anthropologists, *Internationales Asian Forum, International Quarterly for Asian Studies,* 12, Jahrgang, April. Originally published How to Aid Afghan Refugees, in *Royal Anthropological Institute News,* No. 39, August, 1980.

— — — 1981b. Nomadism as Ideological Expression: The Case of the Gomal Nomads. *Nomadic Peoples,* Number 9, September.

— — — 1981c. Review of S.S. Harrison 1981. *Afghanistan Council Newsletter,* September, vol. IX, no. 4. New York: The Asia Society.

———— 1982a. *Muslim Society: Readings in Thought and Structure,* London: Routledge and Kegan Paul.

———— 1982b. Order and Conflict in Muslim Society: A Case Study from Pakistan. *Middle East Journal,* 36(2): 184-204.

———— 1983. *Religion and Politics in Muslim Society: Order and Conflict in Pakistan,* Cambridge University Press.

———— 1984 Al-Biruni: The First Anthropologist, Spring. London: *Royal Anthroplogical Institute News.*

———— *The Social Structure and Organization of Early Muslim Society,* forthcoming book.

———— The Reconsideration of Swat Pathans: A Reply to Fredrik Barth, forthcoming paper.

———— The Man who would be King: British Political Officer among the Bedouin and the Pukhtun, forthcoming paper.

———— and Ahmed Z. 1981. *Tor* and *Mor:* Binary and Opposing Models of Pukhtun Femalehood. T.S. Epstein and S.P.F. Senaratne, eds. *Rural Women: Asian Case-Studies,* Oxford: Pergamon, forthcoming.

———— and Hart, D.M. 1983. *Islam in Tribal Societies: From the Atlas to the Indus,* London: Routledge and Kegan Paul.

———— and Hart, D.M. eds. *Islamic Tribes and European Administrators: Readings in the Colonial Encounter,* forthcoming book.

Ajami, F. 1981. *The Arab Predicament: Arab Political Thought and Practice Since 1967,* Cambridge University Press.

Alavi, H. 1971. The Politics of Dependence: A Village in West Punjab. *South Asian Review,* Vol. 4, No. 2.

———— 1972. Kinship in West Punjab Villages, *Contributions to Indian Sociology,* News Series, No. VI.

Al-Beruni. 1964. *Al-Beruni's India,* edited, notes etc. E.C. Sachau, Vols. 1 & II, Delhi: S. Cahud & Co. Originally published 1888.

Anderson, J. 1981. Review of Ahmed. 1980a. *American Ethnologist,* Vol. 8, No. 2.

Andrae, T. 1936. *Mohammad, the Man and His Faith,* English translation, London.

Antoun, R.T. 1979. *Low-Key Politics: Local-Level Leadership and Change in the Middle East,* Albany: State University of New York Press.

Archer, J.C. 1924. *Mystical Elements in Mohammad,* Yale University Press.

Asad, T. 1972. Market Model, Class Structure and Consent: A Reconsideration of Swat Political Organization. *MAN,* Vol. 7, No. I.

— — — ed. 1973. *Anthropology and the Colonial Encounter,* London: Ithaca Press.

— — — 1975. Anthropological Texts, and Ideological Problems: An Analysis of Cohen on Arab Villages in Israel. *Economy and Society,* Vol. 4, No. 3: 251-82.

Aswad, B.C. 1970. Social and Ecological Aspects in the Formation of Islam. Louise E. Sweet, *ed, Peoples and Cultures of the Middle East,* Vol. I, Garden City, New York: Doubleday and Co. for Natural History Press. 53-73.

Bailey, F.G. 1970. *Stratagems and Spoils,* Oxford: Basil Blackwell.

Banaji, J. 1970. Crisis of British Anthropology. *New Left Review,* No. 64: 71-85.

Barth F. 1961. *Nomads of South Persia: The Basseri Tribe of the Khamseh Confederacy,* London: George Allen and Unwin.

— — — 1966. Models of Social Organization. *Royal Anthropological Institute, Occasional paper* No. 23.

— — — 1972. *Political Leadership among Swat Pathans,* London: Athlone Press.

— — — 1981. *Selected Essays of Fredrik Barth: Features of Person and Society in Swat: Collected Essays on Pathans,* Vol. II, London: Routledge and Kegan Paul.

Beattie, H. 1977. *Other Cultures,* London: Routledge and Kegan Paul.

Bell. R. 1926. *The Origin of Islam in its Christian Environment,* London.

71

Bohannan, P. 1959. The Impact of Money on an African Subsistence Economy. *The Journal of Economic History,* No. 19: 491-503.

Bohannan, P. and Bohannan, L. 1968. *Tiv Economy,* Evanston, Ill. Northwestern University Press.

Bohannan. P. and Dalton, G. eds. 1962. *Markets in Africa,* Evanston, Ill. Northwestern University Press.

Burling, R. 1962. Maximization Theories and the Study of Economic Anthropology. *American Anthropologist,* Vol. 64: 802-21.

Cancian, F. 1966. Maximization as Norm, Strategy and Theory: A Comment on Programmatic Statements in Economic Anthropology. *American Anthropologist,* Vol. 68: 465-70.

Caroe, O. 1965. *The Pathans,* London: Macmillan.

Carpozi, G. Jr. 1979. *Ayatollah Khomeini's Mein Kampf: Islamic Government by Ayatollah Ruhollah Khomeini,* New York: Manor Books.

Chaudhri, N.C. 1965. *The Continent of Circe,* London: Chatto and Windus.

Cole, D. 1975. *Nomads of the Nomads: The Al Murrah Bedouin of the Empty Quarter,* Chicago: Aldine.

Crone, P. and Cook, M. 1980. *Hagarism: The Making of the Islamic World,* Cambridge University Press.

Dalton, G. 1961. Economic Theory and Primitive Society. *American Anthropologist,* Vol. 63, No.1.

— — — 1962. Traditional Production in Primitive African Economies. *The Quarterly Journal of Economics,* 76: 360-78.

— — — 1965. Primitive Money. *American Anthropologist,* Vol. 67: 44-65.

— — — ed. 1967. *Tribal and Peasant Economies: Readings in Economic Anthropology,* New York: Natural History Press.

— — — ed. 1968. *Primitive, Archaic, and Modern Economies: Essays of Karl Polanyi,* New York: Anchor Books.

— — — 1969. Theoretical Issues in Economic Anthropology. *Current Anthropology,* 10: 63-101.

Deane, P. 1953. *Colonial Social Accounting*, Cambridge University Press.

Durkheim, E. 1923. *The Division of Labour*, London.

Eickelman, D.F. 1967. Musaylima: An Approach to the Social Anthropology of Seventh Century Arabia. *Journal of the Economic and Social History of the Orient*, 10: 17-52.

———— 1981. *The Middle East: An Anthropological Approach*. Englewood Cliffs N.J., Prentice-Hall, Inc.

Elphinstone, M. 1972. *An Account of the Kingdom of Caubul*, Vols. I and II, Karachi: Oxford University Press.

El-Zein, A.H.M. 1974. *The Sacred Meadows: A Structural Analysis of Religious Symbolism in an East African Town,* Evanston, Ill: Northwestern University Press.

———— 1977. Beyond Ideology and Theology: The Search for the Anthropology of Islam. *Annual Reviews of Anthropology*, 6: 227-254.

Epstein, T.S. 1962. *Economic Development and Social Change in South India*. Manchester University Press.

Esposito, J.L. ed. 1980. *Islam and Development: Religion and Sociopolitical Change,* Syracuse, New York: Syracuse University Press.

Evans-Pritchard, E.E. 1937. *Witchcraft, Oracles and Magic among the Azande of the Anglo-Egyptian Sudan,* Oxford: Clarendon Press.

———— 1973. *The Sanusi of Cyrenaica,* Oxford University Press.

Faris, J.C. 1973. Pax Britannica and the Sudan: S.F. Nadel. T. Asad, ed. *Anthropology and the Colonial Encounter,* London: Ithaca Press.

Faruqi, I.R.A. 1976 trans. *The Life of Muhammad* by M.H. Haykal, USA: North American Publications.

Firth, R. 1964. Capital, Saving and Credit in Peasant Societies: A view-point from Economic Anthropology. R. Firth and B. Yamey eds. *Capital, Saving and Credit in Peasant Societies,* Chicago: Aldine.

———— 1966. *Malay Fishermen: The Peasant Economy,* London: Routledge and Kegan Paul.

73

——— ed. 1970. *Themes in Economic Anthropology,* ASA Monograph 6, London: Tavistock.

Fischer, M.M.J. 1980. *Iran: From Religious Dispute to Revolution,* Cambridge: Harvard University Press.

Fortes, M. and Evans-Pritchard, E.E. eds. 1970. *African Political Systems,* Oxford University Press.

Freud, S. 1950. *Totem & Taboo,* London.

Gauhar, A. ed. 1978. *The Challenge of Islam,* London: Islamic Council of Europe.

Geertz, C. 1968. *Islam Observed: Religious Development in Morocco and Indonesia,* New Haven and London: Yale University Press.

——— 1973. *The Interpretation of Cultures,* Basic Books, Inc.

Geertz H. and Rosen, L. 1979. *Meaning and Order in Moroccan Society: Three Essays in Cultural Analysis,* Cambridge University Press.

Gellner, E. 1969. *Saints of the Atlas,* London: Weidenfeld and Nicolson.

——— 1981. *Muslim Society,* Cambridge University Press.

Gibb, H.A.R. 1980. *Muhammedanism,* Oxford University Press. First published in the Home University Library (1949).

Godelier, M. 1977. *Perspectives in Marxist Anthropology,* Cambridge University Press.

Grunebaum, Gustave E. von 1951. *Muhammadan Festivals,* New York: Henry Schuman, Inc.

Harrison, S.S. 1981. *In Afghanistan's Shadow: Baluch Nationalism and Soviet Temptations,* Washington and New York: Carnegie Endowment.

Hill, P. 1963. Markets in Africa, *The Journal of Modern African Studies.* Vol. 1, No. 4.

——— 1965. *A Plea for Indigenous Economics: The West African Example,* Economic Development Institute, University of Ibadan.

Hodgson, M.G.S. 1974. *The Venture of Islam,* Chicago: University of Chicago Press.

Jeffrey, P. 1980. *Frogs in a Well*. London: Zed Press.

Khan, M.S. 1980. *Muhammad: Seal of the Prophets*. London: Routledge and Kegan Paul.

Laffin, J. 1981. *The Dagger of Islam*. New York: Bantam Books.

Legace, R.O. 1957. The Formation of the Muslim State. *Anthropology Tomorrow*, The University of Chicago, Vol. 6, No. I: 141-155.

Lancaster, W.O. 1980. Review of Ibrahim and Cole 1978. *Nomadic Peoples* No. 5, Commission on Nomadic Peoples, IUAES.

——— 1981. *The Rawala Bedouin Today*, Berkeley: California University Press.

Laroui, A. 1977. *The History of the Maghrib: An Interpretive Essay,* trans. from French by Ralph Manheim, N.J.: Princeton University Press.

Leach, E.R. 1971 a. *Rethinking Anthropology*, London: Athlone Press.

——— 1971 b. *Aspects of Caste in South India, Ceylon and Northwest Pakistan*, Cambridge University Press.

——— 1977. *Political Systems of Highland Burma: A Study of Kachin Social Structure*, London: Athlone Press.

LeClair, E.E. 1962. Economic Theory and Economic Anthropology. *American Anthropologist*, 64, pp. 1,179-1,203.

——— and Schneider, H.K. eds. 1968. *Economic Anthropology: Readings in Theory and Analysis*, New York: Holt, Rinehart and Winston.

Lewis, B. 1966. *The Arabs in History*, Harper Colophon Books, Harper and Row. Originally published in the History division of Hutchison University Library 1950.

——— 1972. The Study of Islam. *Encounter*, 38, No. 1: 31-34.

Lewis, I.M. 1961. *A Pastoral Democracy*, Oxford University Press.

Lings, M. 1983. *Muhammad*, London: G. Allen and Unwin.

Lyall, A. 1882. *Asiatic Studies: Religious and Social*, London.

Maine, H. 1861. *Ancient Law*, London: John Murray.

— — — 1871. *Village Communities in the East and the West,* London.

Meeker, M.E. 1979. *Literature and Violence in North Arabia.* New York: Cambridge University Press.

Meillasoux, C. 1964. *Anthropologie économique des Gouro de Côte d'Ivoire,* Paris: Mouton.

— — — 1972. From Reproduction to Production: A Marxist Approach to Economic Anthropology. *Economic Society,* Vol. I: 93-105.

Muir, W. 1858-61. *Life of Mohomet,* 4 vols, London.

Naipaul. V.S. 1981. *Among the Believers: An Islamic Journey,* New York: Alfred A. Knopf.

Needham, R. 1970. The Future of Social Anthropology: Disintegration or Metamorphosis?" *Anniversary Contributions to Anthropology: Twelve Essays,* Leiden.

Pastner, C. 1978. Englishmen in Arabia: Encounters with Middle Eastern Women. *Signs: Journal of Women in Culture and Society,* Vol. 4, No. 2. University of Chicago.

Patai, R. 1969. *Society, Culture and Change in the Middle East.* Philadelphia: The University of Pennsylvania Press.

Pehrson, R.N. 1966. *The Social Organization of the Marri Baluch,* compiled and analysed from his notes by Fredrik Barth, Chicago: Viking Fund Publications in Anthropology, No. 43.

Peters, E. 1960. The Proliferation of Segments in the Lineage of the Bedouin of Cyrenaica, *JRAI,* Vol. 90: 29-53.

Polanyi, K. 1944. *The Great Transformation,* New York: Rinehart.

— — — 1966. *Dahomey and the Slave Trade,* Seattle: University of Washington Press.

— — — 1968 a. *Primitive, Archaic, and Modern Economies: Essays of Karl Polanyi,* ed. G. Dalton, New York: Anchor Books, Doubleday.

— — — 1968 b. The Economy as Instituted Process. E.E. LeClair and H.K. Schneider eds. *Economic Anthropology.* New York: Holt, Rinehart and Winston.

— — — Arensberg, C.M. and Pearson, H.W. eds. 1957. *Trade and Market in the Early Empires: Economies in History and Theory,* Glencoe, Ill.: Free Press.

Rahman, F. 1982. The Academic Study of Islam: A Muslim Islamicist's Point of View. R.C. Martin, ed. *Islam and the History of Religions,* Berkeley: University of California Press.

Rey, P.P. 1957. The Lineage Mode of Production. *Critique of Anthropology,* No. 3. London: Spring.

— — — 1980. *Muhammad,* trans. A. Carter, New York: Pantheon Books.

— — — 1981. *The Arabs,* trans. A. Goldhammer, The University of Chicago and Croom Helm, Ltd.

Rodinson, M. 1980. *Muhammad* trans. A. Carter. New York: Pantheon Books.

Sahlins, M.D. 1968. *Tribesmen,* Prentice-Hall for University of Michigan.

— — — 1969. On the Sociology of Primitive Exchange. M. Banton ed. *The Relevance of Models for Social Athropology,* ASA, Monograph No. 1. London: Tavistock.

Said, H.M. ed. 1979. *Al-Beruni: Commemorative Volume,* International Congress. Karachi: Hamdard Academy.

— — — and Zahid, A. 1981. *Al-Beruni, His Times, Life and Works.* Karachi: Hamdard Academy.

Said, W.E. 1978. *Orientalism,* London: Routledge and Kegan Paul.

— — — 1981. *Covering Islam: How the Media and the Experts Determine How We See the Rest of the World,* New York: Pantheon Books.

Shariati, A. 1979. *On the Sociology of Islam: Lectures by Ali Shariati,* trans. H. Algar, Berkeley: Mizan Press.

Southhall, A.W. 1953. *Alur Society,* Cambridge: W. Heffer.

Tapper, R. 1979. *Pasture and Politics: Economics, Conflict and Ritual among Shahsevan Nomads of Northwestern Iran,* New York: Academic Press.

——— 1981. Review of Ahmed 1980. *Asian Affairs,* Vol. 12 Pt. B, October, London.

Terray, E. 1972. *Marxism and Primitive Societies: Two Studies,* New York: Monthly Review Press.

——— 1975 a. Technology, Tradition and the State. *Critique of Anthropology,* No. 3, Spring, London.

——— 1975 b. Classes and Class Consciousness in the Abron Kingdom of Gyaman. In M. Bloch, (ed.), *Marxist Analyses and Social Anthropology,* London: Malaby Press.

Thaiss, G. 1978. Religious Symbolism and Social Change: The Drama of Husain. N.R. Keddie, ed. *Scholars, Saints, and Sufis,* Berkeley: University of California Press.

Tidrick, K. 1981. *Heart-Beguiling Araby,* Cambridge University Press.

Turner, B.S. 1974. *Weber and Islam: A Critical Study,* London: Routledge and Kegan Paul.

Tylor, E.B. 1871. *Primitive Culture,* London.

Vincent, J. 1978. Political Anthropology: Manipulative Strategies. *Annual Reviews of Anthropology,* 7: 175-94.

Watt, W.M. 1953. *Muhammad at Mecca,* Oxford: Clarendon Press.

——— 1956. *Muhammad at Medina,* Oxford: Clarendon Press.

——— 1978. *Muhammad: Prophet and Statesman,* Oxford University Press. First published by Clarendon Press, 1961.

Wax, R.H. 1971. *Doing Fieldwork, Warning and Advice,* Chicago and London: University of Chicago Press.

Wi kan. U. 1977. Mana Becomes Women: Transsexualism in Oman as a Key to Gender Roles. *Man* (N.S.). Vol 12, No. 2, August.

Winter, E.H. 1973. Territorial Grouping and Religion Among the Iraqw. M. Banton ed. *Anthropological Approaches to the Study of Religion,* ASA Monograph No. 3, London: Tavistock.

Wittfogel, K. 1957. *Oriental Despotism: A Comparative Study of Total Power,* Yale University Press. Paperback version (1981). New York: Vintage Books.

Wolf, E. 1951. The Social Organization of Mecca and the Origins of Islam. *South-Western Journal of Anthropology,* No. 7, Winter 329-56.